A JOHN BOSWELL ASSOCIATES BOOK

Simon and Schuster

NEW YORK

LONDON

TORONTO

SYDNEY

TOKYO

The Best of Everything

·····························

The Insider's Guide
to Collecting — for
Every Taste and
Every Budget

JOHN L. MARION

CHAIRMAN OF SOTHEBY'S, INC.

with Christopher Andersen

Simon and Schuster
Simon & Schuster Building
Rockefeller Center
1230 Avenue of the Americas
New York, New York 10020

Copyright © 1989 by John L. Marion and John Boswell

All rights reserved
including the right of reproduction
in whole or in part in any form.

SIMON AND SCHUSTER and colophon are registered trademarks
of Simon & Schuster Inc.

Designed by Liney Li
Manufactured in the United States of America

1   3   5   7   9   10   8   6   4   2

Library of Congress Cataloging-in-Publication Data
Marion, John L.
The best of everything: the insider's guide to collecting—
for every taste and every budget/John L. Marion, with Christopher Andersen.
p.   cm.
"A John Boswell Associates book"—P. opp. t. p.
1. Collectibles as an investment.   2. Antiques as an investment.
3. Collectors and collecting—History—20th century.
4. Sotheby's (Firm)   5. Auctions.
I. Andersen, Christopher P.   II. Title.
AM237.M37   1989
332.63—dc20   *89-21673*
                                                           CIP

ISBN 0-671-66783-1

Acknowledgments

IN our search for *The Best of Everything* we were fortunate to have the guidance and encouragement of many people, both inside and outside the collecting field. First, we owe a special debt of gratitude to our editor, Frederic W. Hills, to John Boswell, who initially conceived the project, and to Jennifer Brown, who acted as its catalyst.

Our thanks also to William S. Paley, Malcolm Forbes, Bill Cosby, Sally Ganz, and Ellen Levine for their wisdom, and to the entire staff at Sotheby's for their advice and cooperation, including John D. Block, Diana D. Brooks, Barbara Deisroth, Nancy Druckman, Anthony Grant, Dana Hawkes, Diana Levitt, Lucy Mitchell-Innes, David J. Nash, Peter Rathbone, George Read, Letitia Roberts, Laura Stewart, Kevin L. Tierney, and George Wachter.

To Anne and "our" children:

John, Jr.

Debbie

Windi

Teri

and Michelle

Contents

Introduction

WHEN I started out in the auction business nearly thirty years ago, news of record sales was relegated to the back pages of *The New York Times*. Today, sales figures are often so astronomical —roughly $50 million each for van Gogh's *Irises* and the Duchess of Windsor's jewelry collection, just to name two examples—that they land on page one.

For most people, these headlines have underscored what most of us long assumed to be the case—that collecting is, has been, and always will be a game for the very rich. There is some truth to this. The prices for old master and Impressionist master-pieces have been pushed out of sight, certainly. But it is just as important to realize that *tomorrow's* masterpieces are within your grasp *today*.

Every day more and more people are learning the collecting world's "biggest little secret": that there are extraordinary, *af-fordable* opportunities out there, and that you don't have to be a king—or even a corporate raider—to take advantage of them. What they often don't know is how to go about taking advantage of those opportunities.

I hope that even world-class connoisseurs will learn some-thing from reading this book, though it was not primarily for them that it was written. *The Best of Everything* takes the mystery out of collecting. It is the first book to give aspiring connoisseurs all the information, insights, and strategies they need to put them on an equal footing with more experienced collectors.

Obviously, nobody can learn to become an expert overnight. What can be learned quickly is the methodology—my systemized approach—for developing an eye for quality. You will find all you need to know in the following pages. All you have to do is bring your passion.

Investing in beautiful things is not only a smart way to allocate one's assets, it can also be one of life's great joys. From flea markets, garage sales, and antiques shops to big-city galleries and the world's great auction houses, collecting has become America's number one indoor sport. *The Best of Everything* can help anyone become not only a player but a champion.

CHAPTER — ONE

There's a Little Bit of Andy in All of Us

 Not long after Andy Warhol's death in 1987, his executors approached Sotheby's and asked us to auction off the contents of his estate. I had known Andy—if anybody could really claim to know Andy Warhol—for years, but when I first walked into his six-story Manhattan town house I was stunned by what I found: room after darkened room literally crammed to the ceiling with more than ten thousand items he had collected over the years, many stuffed in closets or sealed in cardboard boxes that Warhol had never even bothered to open.

Predictably, there were outstanding examples of modern and contemporary art—works by Picasso, Edvard Munch, Marcel Duchamp, Jasper Johns, Robert Rauschenberg, and Roy Lichten-

stein—as well as some of the finest examples of Art Deco furniture and jewelry anywhere. And, as might have been expected
from the man who made Brillo pads and Campbell's soup cans
icons of the age, Andy had squirreled away the world's greatest
collection of kitsch: cigar store Indians, Victorian shoes, carousel
horses, toy soldiers, Eskimo bone masks, World War II medals,
battery-powered space toys, quilts, tomahawks, 175 cookie jars,
313 watches, Superman telephones, piles of Navaho and Pueblo
blankets, Miss Piggy and Kermit the Frog beach towels, prehis-
toric pottery, a bagful of high school graduation rings, and
enough Fiestaware to serve the customers of a fair-size roadside
diner.

The few rooms in his East Sixty-sixth Street town house that
were in fact habitable revealed a side to Warhol that came as a
complete surprise. The king of Pop Art, it turned out, also had
amassed a truly important collection of American classical and
Federal furnishings—eighteenth- and nineteenth-century beds,
mirrors, desks, chairs, tables, silver flatware, and tea sets. Abstract, yes, and Art Deco, maybe . . . but who could have guessed
Andy would have had such a consuming passion for Early American?

Ultimately, of course, our sale of the Warhol collection in the
spring of 1988 turned out to be an event in itself. More than
fifteen thousand collectors swarmed to see the 3,436 lots, and
many were willing to pay whatever it would take for a piece of
Warhol mystique. A $20 Fred Flintstone quartz watch never taken
out of its box fetched over $2,000. A pair of salt and pepper
shakers went for $23,100—more than *two hundred times* what
we estimated they would sell for in our catalogue. As for Andy's
collection of kitschy cookie jars, we valued each at between $25
and $150 for a total of $7,000. One New York businessman
bought no fewer than 136 of them for the mind-spinning sum of
$198,605! (The entire batch went for $247,000.) All in all, the ten-
day-long auction extravaganza totaled a little over $25.3 million
—nearly twice what we had predicted.

The Warhol sale was nothing less, as *Time* magazine put it, than the "Garage Sale of the Century." But, more than any other art event in recent memory, it also served to illustrate the fact that man is by nature an acquisitive animal. We all value objects we can touch and feel and appreciate, and usually these are the things we wish to possess.

Thank goodness, even among pack rats few are as compulsive about hoarding as Andy Warhol was. Yet there is a little bit of Andy in all of us. Like him, we all dream of that elusive $10 find that turns out to be worth $1 million. We will probably never make that discovery (I use the word "probably" advisedly here, since I have seen more than my share of "miracle finds" over the years), but that doesn't mean we can't have a hell of a lot of fun trying—and make a considerable profit in the bargain.

No, You Don't Have to Be Rich

A few years ago, one of my Connecticut neighbors called to say that he was on his way to an Oriental rug sale "out by the airport." Did I, he asked, have any last-minute "tips" for him?

"Yes," I said, "don't go. There's a very good reason that sale is being held at the airport, you know. Why not come to Sotheby's? We have a great rug auction coming up next month."

"Oh, I could never afford the prices you get there," he replied.

I told him he was likely to pay no more at Sotheby's than he was at that airport sale, but it was clear that he didn't quite believe what I was saying. This, in fact, is a reaction I get all the time. Most people think you have to be a millionaire to own fine art and precious antiques.

To be sure, collecting can be expensive—often frighteningly so. Most of the auctions anyone reads about in the newspapers are, of course, sales of the rarest and costliest pieces. When I gaveled down van Gogh's *Irises* in 1987 for $49 million ($53.9 million when you include Sotheby's fee), for example, it was trumpeted on front pages across the globe as the highest price ever paid at auction for a work of art. (That figure was almost topped in the spring of 1989 when a Picasso self-portrait brought $47.9 million.) Such record-breaking auctions—and there have been many in recent years—are obviously welcome in my business. But they do tend to distort reality, leading to the unfortunate assumption that all fine art is priced far beyond the reach of the average person.

In truth, there has been a vast change in the nature of the average collector over the past twenty years. Once you had to be one of The 400—the very few, very lucky people with real means. Today the average person in the suburbs is likely to be a serious collector of something—stamps, perhaps, or old bottles or buttons or antique cars, but *something*. (I have even encountered people who collect barbed wire, but that's a different story.) My father traveled a great deal, and the tiny soaps he brought back from luxury hotels around the country made up my very first collection. Lots of boys collected stamps or baseball cards, but I'm pretty sure I was the only kid in our neighborhood who collected soap.

A great many genuine antiques are available for prices that are on a par or only slightly higher than their modern-day reproductions. Certainly, rare and exceptionally fine works are expensive, but it is precisely because they are so rare that this is so. The majority—and this invariably comes as a surprise to the average person—*are quite affordable.* Keep in mind that the genuine article has a resale value on the open market unmatched by any reproduction—no matter how skillfully crafted.

So, as I asked my friend headed for that airport rug auction, why pay for something of dubious quality? With the proper guidance, you can have the real thing—like the exquisite eight-foot by four-foot 1920s Persian rug we sold for $1,980, or about half what you might pay at Bloomingdale's or Macy's for a new rug of comparable quality.

Buy for Love and Money: But First for Love

Just how strong is today's art and collectibles market? In 1988, we at Sotheby's alone sold art and collectibles worth $1.814 *billion*—ranging from Warhol and the private collection of Elton John ($8.175 million) to a love letter written by Abraham Lincoln before he married Mary Todd ($77,000), an extremely rare Guarneri violin ($1 million), and a handwritten manuscript in which Albert Einstein first outlined his theory of relativity, including the equation $EL = MC^2$ with the "L" hastily crossed out ($1.15 million).

That year there were also record sales in areas that do not always land on the front page, such as photographs, prints, antiquities, rugs, American furniture and paintings, English ceramics, Chinese porcelain, tribal art, Islamic art, and even rock-and-roll memorabilia.

In 1988 we auctioned five lots for over $10 million each and 134 more for over $1 million. In the course of just three days in November of that year, I auctioned Impressionist and modern paintings worth $200 million. But we also sold *190,000 lots for under $10,000*—and that is the figure most worth remembering.

Suddenly there is a tremendous thirst for the tangible in this country, and with good reason. Over the past few years the stock market has left an awful lot of scar tissue on the average investor. So Americans are doing what Europeans have done for centuries—they're looking for an investment that is portable, beautiful, a reminder of their cultural heritage, and a hedge against inflation. As long as people need to preserve the value of their capital, they will seek out scarce objects. The market for those objects can continue in only one direction: up.

Almost without exception, if you had bought any piece of fine

This exquisite Sarouk
Fereghan Persian rug, circa 1920, sold for
$1,980 at auction—a superb value.

Einstein's original manuscript
outlining his E = mc² Theory of Relativity,
sold at Sotheby's for $1.55 million.
Note the hastily crossed-out "L."

art or quality collectible in, say, the last three decades, it would have proved to be a wise investment. Maybe even a spectacular one. In 1952, my father, Louis J. Marion, then chief auctioneer of Parke-Bernet Galleries in New York, auctioned the *Farewell of Telemachus and Eucharis* by Jacques-Louis David for $3,950. Thirty-five years later, I sold the same painting to the Getty Museum for *$4,070,000*—then a record for a nineteenth-century European painting.

Degas's bronze figure of a dancer, *Petite Danseuse à quatorze ans,* was panned by critics when it was first shown, at the 1881 Impressionist exhibition in Paris. One described the little dancer as "an unhappy child, ugly, and with a profoundly vicious character." Another went so far as to write, "God forbid my daughter should become a dancer." Purchased in 1971 for $380,000, the "ugly" little Degas dancer was sold in May of 1988 for $10,120,000—another record, this one for a sculpture at auction.

Painting and sculpture are just two of the areas where a collector could have made a veritable killing in recent years. A page from an illuminated manuscript of the Jewish Haggadah, circa 1736, was sold in 1970 for $13,500. In 1983. the same page fetched $290,400 at auction—at 2,000 percent profit in just thirteen years. In the area of folk art, a carved wooden figure of a racetrack tout dating from 1870 went for $31,900 in 1979. Just one year later, it was sold at Sotheby's for $58,300.

On a more down-to-earth scale, the bottle of Château Latour you bought in 1970 for $65 may now be worth over $1,000, and the original celluloid (cel) from Walt Disney's *Dumbo* that you picked up along with a Davy Crockett coonskin cap for under $10 on a 1964 trip to the Magic Kingdom could bring you upward of $5,000 today.

Enticing, yes, but keep in mind the following: Collecting is a way to add to the quality of your life. If you go about it in the right way, you will do very well financially. If, on the other hand, financial gain is your *primary* motive for collecting, chances are

*This carved wooden figure of
a racetrack tout nearly doubled in value from
$31,900 to $58,300 in a single year.*

A celluloid
from the Walt Disney
classic Dumbo

you will lose in the long run. You will fail because you will be buying art for all the wrong reasons. This is one of the delicious ironies that make the collector's world unlike any other, and there are basically two reasons for it. First, it takes time and no small degree of commitment to acquire an eye for quality. People who are simply looking for a quick turnaround on their investment—in plainer English, the proverbial fast buck—will never devote the time it takes to develop the necessary depth of understanding.

Conversely, people who are passionately involved as collectors are insatiably curious about their chosen field—whether it be old master paintings or coins or paperweights or movie posters. They absorb knowledge like a sponge. Even though he may have less money to spend at the outset than his fast-buck counterpart, the involved, knowledgeable collector will always have the upper hand.

Second, and this is more obvious, the self-educated collector is often in a position to see what others cannot. Several years ago, a woman brought in a "sweetmeats" dish that she had purchased at a garage sale for $4. It was not very interesting to look at—you and I might well have left it in the garage. By reading books and prowling museums, this woman happened to have learned quite a bit about American porcelain and had a pretty good idea of what she had come across. Still, even our experts at Sotheby's had to catch their breath when the sweetmeats dish bought for $4 at a garage sale sold at auction for $66,000—a record at the time for American porcelain. The dish, which measures about six inches in diameter, is now on display in the American wing of New York's Metropolitan Museum of Art.

Treasures at a Tag Sale

A graphic example of the educated collector's advantage occurred in May of 1988, when a commercial fisherman who happened to collect rare books was browsing through a bin of early-twentieth-century farm pamphlets in a southern New Hampshire barn-turned-antiques-store. The man spotted a frayed, stained forty-page pamphlet entitled *Tamerlane and Other Poems,* attributed only to "A Bostonian." The man had recognized the title from an article he had just read in *Yankee Bookseller* magazine, and paid the antiques barn's $15 asking price. When the man was told by our rare books expert in Boston that he had stumbled upon the twelfth known copy of Edgar Allan Poe's first volume of poetry (published in 1827, when Poe was just fourteen), the poor fellow passed out cold. A few months later we sold the slim volume for $198,000.

Unearthing a first edition of the first book by the man believed by some to be America's greatest author is the Holy Grail of book collecting. Even though the fortunate collector had been at it for only three years and had in fact never before read anything by Poe, he had so immersed himself in his field that he could recognize a true gem in the unlikeliest of settings.

Such discoveries are far from frequent, but they do happen —and they happen every year. At a swap meet held in a garage next to our Los Angeles office in 1980, we came across a Fabergé enamel box with a $20 price tag. We sold the box for $5,000 then, and it would fetch ten times that today. On another occasion, an elderly lady came into Sotheby's New York headquarters with a shopping bag full of things, including a big clock she thought was worth a fortune. The clock turned out to be worth $150. Then, as an afterthought, she pulled a dirty old Russian enamel tankard out of her sack. We appraised it at $15,000 on the spot as a piece from the Fabergé workshop.

From "junk" to treasure:
A rare Medici porcelain used as
a sugar bowl by nuns at a convent
in Yonkers sold for a record $180,000.

*A secretary found
this Han dynasty pottery
dog in a shoebox
full of knickknacks.
It sold for $5,250.*

A couple brought this T'ang pottery
figure in to be appraised during our
free "Heirloom Discovery Days."
It brought $92,500—another record.

*A delivery boy cashed
in a pawn ticket for $50,000 worth
of antiques and silver—
including this rare Italian
Valadier tray that was
auctioned for $8,250.*

A copy of Edgar Allan Poe's Tamerlane
purchased at a barn sale for $15 in
May 1988 brought $198,000 a few months later.

Sometimes these sensational finds have a ripple effect. One man came in with an old painting that had been in his family for years. It was by the sixteenth-century Flemish old master Brueghel the Elder, and we sold it at auction for $560,000. Another fellow read about that sale, saw a photograph of the painting in the newspaper, and came to us with a still life he said looked as if it might have come from the school of Brueghel. It, too, turned out to be by the artist himself. It went for $410,000. Again, these sales occurred a few years ago; both paintings, had their owners held on to them, would be worth several times that today.

Frankly, I find even more modest (if that's the right word) discoveries exciting: the Tlingit Indian dagger found in a Scarsdale attic that sold for $72,000, for example, and the fifteenth-century blue and white floral Ming dynasty dish once purchased for $6 and toted into Sotheby's in a brown paper bag—it brought $76,000. I once auctioned for $180,000 a rare Medici porcelain cup that had been used as a sugar bowl at a convent in Yonkers. Even that must take a back seat to the exquisite Ming copperglazed vase that sold for $1,438,462 in May of 1987. Not long before, its owner had been using the world's costliest piece of Ming pottery as a bedroom table lamp!

Do these finds sound a little like winning the lottery? Actually, the sensation is even greater, because collecting is in itself a passionate art. The collector gets excited not so much by the monetary value of what he collects as by its intrinsic value. He lives with an object, derives pleasure from it, wraps himself and his psyche around it. The thrill may come from discovering new details in a painting you have just purchased or—better yet— one that has been hanging on your wall for years. Or, if you are more tactilely inclined, there is real pleasure to be had from picking up that object you have come to love, feeling its weight and its texture, and wondering who has held and cherished this very same object before.

The payoff need not always be as spectacular as the sweet-

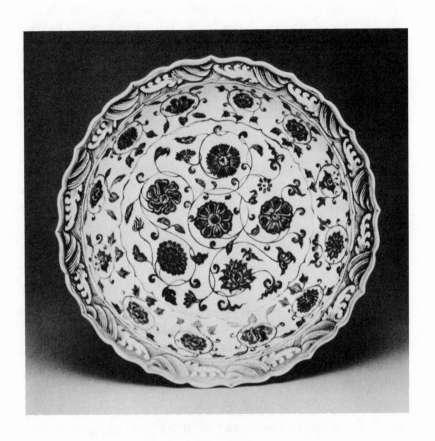

*This Ming dynasty
dish picked up for $6
at an auction was sold
for $76,000 in 1980.*

meats dish or the Edgar Allan Poe pamphlet. The mother of a friend spotted what she thought were two Steuben glass urns amidst the tacky ceramic knickknacks in the window of a thrift shop in rural Shingle Springs, California. On closer examination, she saw that indeed the pieces were signed "Steuben," but that still wasn't enough to convince her. She did some additional research at the local library and, at last satisfied that these were the real thing, bought the two urns for $100. She then sent a Polaroid snapshot of the urns to Steuben headquarters in New York, and was told that the urns were manufactured about 1920 and appraised at just under $500—nearly five times what she paid for them. That value has increased further in the past two years. Not that she's selling. The savvy collector bought them, she says, because she loves the look and feel of fine glass, in particular the artistry of Steuben.

A photography buff paid one dollar for a dusty, worn album of old photographs he unearthed at a suburban tag sale. The quiet, reflective pictures turned out to be the work of Eugene Atget, the French photographer famous for his Paris street scenes. Several months later, the photo album was auctioned for the considerable sum of $16,000.

It is this thrill of discovery that I love most about collecting: the idea that you can still unearth a treasure—even if it's only a small one—at a tag sale. But if you are really going to be a successful collector, you must be willing to make the emotional investment. There are simply too many people out there—your prospective competition—who are obsessed by their "hobby." Once again, those who are in it just for the money will always be at a decided disadvantage.

The Magic Sewing Table

At times, luck takes over completely. Which brings me back to the curious tale of Andy's secret stash. Two months after the Warhol auction, which included the sale of jewelry worth nearly $2 million, curators were moving two file cabinets at Andy's Manhattan town house when they discovered yet another cache, hidden away in the false bottom of a drawer. The incredible find included a small gold pillbox filled with 72 loose diamonds (including one seven-carat emerald-cut diamond worth about $150,000), as well as scores of sapphires, 20 diamond solitaire engagement rings, 96 watches by Rolex, Cartier, and Patek Philippe, and designer pieces by Schlumberger and Elsa Peretti—and the pièce de résistance: a 300-carat carved emerald. What almost wound up in the trash eventually brought another $1.64 million at auction, the proceeds of which went to the Andy Warhol Foundation for the Visual Arts.

As strange as the Case of the Mysteriously Reappearing Jewelry might seem, it was not entirely without precedent. In 1979, I had the great personal satisfaction of being the auctioneer for the art and antiques collections of the late Edgar and Bernice Chrysler Garbisch—two incredible collectors who will be discussed at some length later in this book. Shortly before the Garbisch sale, I was visiting Pokety Farms, their estate on Chesapeake Bay, and for some reason was drawn to a little Salem sewing table tucked away in the corner of the Garbisches' master bedroom. I pulled out the top drawer, pushed aside some yarn, and out came a ring. So I removed the drawer and emptied the contents out on the bed: eight pieces of David Webb–designed jewelry, including a four-carat emerald-cut pink diamond—the most expensive diamond per carat ever sold up until that time. Total value of the newly discovered jewelry: nearly $400,000.

A month and a half later, I returned to Pokety Farms with a reporter. When I spotted the little Salem sewing table in the corner of the Garbisches' bedroom, I couldn't resist. The drawers were empty by now, of course, but I poked my hand down into the little basket that hung under the table and—up popped a bracelet! When I got back to New York, I called the executors of the Garbisch estate again. "Hey, guess what happened? I found another bracelet in that table!"

Naturally, I now own that table. Couldn't have it any other way. And I keep looking in that damn drawer and basket. Nothing! Which goes to prove that, in the collecting game, you can't count on lucky discoveries—but they are marvelous when they happen.

Decorating Your Cave

How do novice collectors get started? Obviously, they must first define what it is that they want to collect—what appeals most strongly to their aesthetic sense. From there on, becoming a knowledgeable collector requires that the individual go through a process of self-education. That means visiting museums and galleries, attending auctions, reading what is available on the specific areas he or she has chosen, consulting the experts, and other techniques we will discuss at length a bit later on. This ultimately leads, in the best of all possible worlds, to a refinement of taste and a sophistication of choice that are the hallmarks of the bona fide collector.

Now that I have said this, the unvarnished truth is that most people, myself included, are invariably motivated to become collectors for more mundane reasons. Namely—an empty room, a naked wall, a sprawling space on a table that calls for something to fill it up. In short, most of us are simply in the process of decorating or redecorating our homes.

This is hardly a recent development. Cave paintings have been around for almost as long as man has been around to paint them. The pharaohs of ancient Egypt took things a step further. Convinced that you *can* take it with you, they were entombed surrounded by their treasures, with the intent of carrying them along on their voyage to the afterlife. The desire to make one's surroundings as aesthetically pleasing as possible is older than recorded time; it is hard to imagine that anything could be more indelibly imprinted in our species' genetic code.

THERE'S A LITTLE BIT OF ANDY IN ALL OF US

My own introduction to collecting antiquities had its origins a few years ago in just such a dilemma. I had purchased a chest of drawers and wanted to cover the top with something other than a vase of flowers or family photographs. A little diversion, if you will. Collecting antiquities is such a pleasure—a privilege, really—that looking back I am ashamed to confess that what I was after was a set of attractive and inexpensive knickknacks to fill up a space. My solution was to buy at Sotheby's a "mixed lot": a small Roman statue, a piece of terra-cotta pottery, the finial from a statue, and a couple of other items. The total cost of all these remnants of great civilizations came to a modest $200. Not only was the price right, but this grab-bag approach saved me the bother of putting together a collection of antiquities single piece by single piece.

When I got home, I carefully took all the pieces out of the cardboard box in which they came, arranged them on the top of the chest, adjusted the lighting to best show them off, and then walked away. What I failed to realize at the time, of course, is that there is something almost sacred about an object that is thousands of years old; it simply demands your attention. I found myself mysteriously beckoned by these antiquities, and I wondered about the families that owned them before me.

This ultimately led (as it often does) to an almost obsessive preoccupation not only with collecting antiquities but with the ancient cultures and dynasties from which they come. I like to think that, by degrees, I have become at least somewhat knowledgeable about the field.

As a result, my appetite for antiquities increased. After covering my chest of drawers, a coffee table, a couple of end tables, and nearly every other flat surface in my home, I decided it was time to buy a lighted mahogany case where my rapidly growing collection could be properly displayed. My little treasure chest has since expanded to include a 2,300-year-old Egyptian bust, a Han dynasty horse, several Art Deco bronzes, two Balinese dancing figures, a few Pre-Columbian pieces, and a family of thumbnail-size ceramic puppies I picked up at a motel gift shop in eastern Maryland—for a little historical perspective.

Now that my mahogany display case is full to overflowing, I have adopted a more disciplined buying policy. Before I buy another piece, it must first meet this criterion: it must be good enough to replace an object already in my collection. This new policy has not only slowed down my acquisitions but made me a more selective collector. Therein lies an important lesson for the novice who feels compelled to buy everything in sight. It is self-discipline that makes the aspiring collector more targeted and, ultimately, more discerning.

Don't Be an Unguided Missile

There are basically two types of collectors: the *furnisher* (also known as the accumulator) and the true collector, or *connoisseur*. Not long ago I gave a speech to a group of American corporate presidents meeting in Hong Kong. One of the topics discussed was the Chinese art market—in particular the tremendous opportunities that lie ahead for those buyers who invest in antique Chinese tables and chairs. (Ironically, Taiwan is as interesting a place as either Hong Kong or the People's Republic to look for Chinese art and antiques of the highest caliber. When Chiang Kai-shek and the Nationalists left the mainland after the Communist revolution in 1949 and headed for Taiwan, they took plenty with them.)

Two days after my speech to the American executives, we were preparing to leave Hong Kong when one of the CEOs walked up, pumped my hand, and thanked me profusely.

"For what?" I asked, understandably confused, since I had never even met this fellow.

"Why," he answered, to my abject horror, "for giving us that great tip on the Oriental furniture. My wife and I went out and bought a whole houseful. We're getting rid of all our English and American antiques back home and replacing them with Chinese stuff!"

A prototypical furnisher, this man fired off like an unguided missile, spending thousands of dollars on Chinese antiques without having a clue as to their quality. Thank God he could easily afford to throw away his money, because, without taking the time and the care to cultivate at least a passing acquaintance with the field of Chinese furnishings, that may well be precisely what he did.

Not that some furnishers don't make wise choices. On the contrary. One wealthy gentleman who had recently bought a house in Stamford, Connecticut, was such an active bidder at so many of our auctions that over the course of a year he became something of a fixture at Sotheby's. After one particularly spirited auction, at which he outbid several antiques dealers for a pair of eagle consoles, I congratulated him. As he left, I waved good-bye.

"See you next week."

"I won't be back," he replied.

"Why not?"

"Well, I filled the house. This pair of consoles I bought today to go in the hallway were the last things I needed."

Now, that is definitely not a collector. *That* is a furnisher—someone motivated not so much by any aesthetic sense as by the understandable need to beautify his or her surroundings with reliable "brand names." A few fall into the trap of collecting what some of my colleagues call *junque*. No matter how you spell it, that is precisely the right word to describe mediocre works bought for inordinately large sums. Nevertheless, that doesn't mean furnishers are any less likely to revel in their acquisitions.

The ultimate furnisher was none other than the legendary press lord William Randolph Hearst, who paid a global army of agents millions to find and dismantle entire European palaces only to have them and their contents shipped across the Atlantic and reassembled at San Simeon, his fabled Xanadu on the California coast. What did not find a home in San Simeon filled more than seven warehouses.

Hearst met his match in Francis P. Garvan, a pioneer aficionado of Americana, who employed his own scouts to ferret out hidden treasures. At one auction in the 1940s, Hearst's agent and Garvan's agent met head to head in a battle over a half-dozen antique copper pots. Each wanted the pots, valued at about $100, and each had virtually carte blanche to get them. Once the bidding for the copper pots reached the absurdly high figure of $7,000 with no end in sight, Major Parke, the auctioneer, abruptly stopped the proceedings and withdrew the pots from the sale.

Imagine what would have transpired had the pots gone up to $30,000 before one of the two bidders dropped out. The "winner" would in all likelihood have been fired by his boss for spending $30,000 on kitchen pots, and the "loser" would have been fired for *not* spending $30,000 for the pots. By calling a halt to the insanity, Major Parke probably saved both men's jobs. (Eventually, the pots found their way into Hearst's hands. They still hang on the kitchen wall at San Simeon, shiny symbols of the mind-boggling lengths to which a determined accumulator will go.)

The Connoisseur

As ironic as it may sound, no one in my family was ever a serious collector—this despite the fact that my father was in the auction business for nearly half a century. I wasn't either, at least not until I reached my twenties (my interest in antiquities, as I noted, came much later). It was then, in 1961, that I accompanied my father on a trip to Easton, Maryland, to appraise the Reginald Lewis estate prior to its coming to auction. Lewis, who had made his fortune on Wall Street, amassed what was reputed to be one of the finest collections of American furniture and Currier & Ives prints anywhere.

For me, just walking through the door was a revelation. I understood for the first time how it all worked together to create an ambiance—from the classic Chesapeake Bay architecture of the mansion itself down to the silverware on the table. The man truly *lived* with his antiques. He'd put his feet up on an eighteenth-century Chippendale cherrywood footstool in the library, eaten off George Washington's china, and kept his shirts in a pre–Revolutionary War chest of drawers. Just by looking at these wonderful pieces, you could get a pretty good idea of what kind of man lived here. That day marked the beginning of my love affair with American furniture and decorations.

No one knew better than Reginald Lewis that the road to connoisseurship is an exciting and tremendously fulfilling one. It is this experience that binds collectors together. Nevertheless, the connoisseurs are by no means a homogeneous group. There are distinct differences within the ranks of the connoisseurs themselves. These variations in taste can run along national, regional, ethnic, even gender lines.

The Germans—an important force because of the strength of the mark—prefer Expressionists like Ernst Ludwig Kirchner, Emil Nolde, and Gustav Klimt. The Japanese have become major players over the past fifteen years, eagerly buying up Chinese and Japanese art, jewelry, and French painters, particularly Renoir (their favorite), van Gogh, Monet, Manet, Degas, and Utrillo. Collectors from the Middle East gravitate toward glitter —porcelains, jewelry, nineteenth-century gold boxes, classic automobiles. To the Arabs, though, the real excitement comes not so much from discovering a wonderful and rare object as it does from the bidding itself; they consider an auction to be an afternoon well spent, like a game of roulette. Like many of us, they enjoy the action.

It's fairly easy to tell an American's general area of interest just on the basis of outward appearances. A couple walks into Sotheby's in New York. He is wearing a pinstripe suit, and her jewelry is nothing short of exquisite. They are probably here to look at the Impressionist paintings, or perhaps eighteenth-century French furnishings.

Let's say she is sporting a pageboy haircut, a black smock, and large, clunky earrings. He is clad in a turtleneck and a blazer. Modern and contemporary art, I would say. Almost certainly Art Nouveau or Art Deco. Maybe folk art as well. If they drive a Land Rover and have a penchant for sweaters and jeans, we may be talking American paintings or collectibles—movie posters, juke-boxes, perhaps some pieces of jewelry from the 1930s and 1940s. Tweeds and a station wagon? Hunting prints, books, silver, and English furniture, old master prints, duck decoys for sure. Stereo-types may go as the market expands. But for now, appearances are seldom deceiving.

The Gender Factor

At the obvious risk of sounding flagrantly sexist, I must point out that there is a significant gender gap when it comes to the things women and men collect and how they go about collecting. Women, for example, tend to be more visually stimulated. Impressionist paintings, French furniture, jewelry, fine silver, and crystal attract at least as many female collectors as male.

Men still dominate the field when it comes to collecting old master paintings, rare books and manuscripts, coins, stamps, and English and American furniture. They are more hands-on in their approach. The next time you are in an antiques store or auction gallery, just watch the way a woman steps back to study the look of a piece of furniture from a distance. A man, on the other hand, is usually more tactile. He opens and shuts the drawers, then runs his fingers over the finish, admiring the feel, the texture of the wood. As an avid collector of Federal furniture myself, I can identify with the pieces I buy. That, I believe, is true of most of my male colleagues.

Women, however, tend to work harder than men at becoming educated collectors. They dig more deeply, read more extensively, take more courses; in short, they do their homework. At most of my lectures women invariably outnumber the men two to one. Women are less likely to take the plunge without first dipping in their little toe.

Men, on the other hand, are sometimes so fiercely competitive that they barely take the time to check if there is water in the pool at all. This is what I call the gender factor, and it can drive the price for even a modest work through the roof. One evening in 1973, I was selling a painting by the Japanese-American artist Yasuo Kuniyoshi. The presale estimate was $15,000 to $20,000. I was calling bids when all of a sudden I realized we had gotten up to *$200,000*. I thought to myself, "Can this be right? In just a moment there will be trouble—someone in the audience will protest." But a Japanese gentleman in the front row was nodding his head, and when I called $220,000 as the final bid, he smiled triumphantly. Of course, this reflects Japanese interest in a Japanese-American artist. But just as important, we are seeing the gender factor at work: this bidder was willing to pay ten times the estimated value of the painting to defeat the competition. We set a world record for the artist back then, but frankly, I doubt if the same painting would fetch much more than the original $20,000 if it were put on the market today.

Whatever his or her particular subspecies, every connoisseur shares the same underlying addiction to the thrill of discovery. For in a very real sense, collecting is a treasure hunt—a search for the beautiful, the ephemeral, the rare—that can turn you into the Sherlock Holmes of American Centennial furniture or the Miss Marple of paperweights.

If you worry that you are somehow not cut out to be a connoisseur, don't. Are you a sports fan—a baseball, football, basketball, tennis, or golf fanatic? Or maybe food—be it haute cuisine or barbecue—is your particular passion. Chances are you already qualify as a connoisseur of something, and whether you are aware of it or not, you already have the right stuff to become a true collector.

But are there any real bargains left out there? Consider this: On April 10, 1886, the American Art Association of the City of New York sponsored the first showing of French Impressionist paintings in this country, featuring the works of Manet, Monet, Renoir, Paul Signac, Georges Seurat, Camille Pissarro, and Degas. The show was an unmitigated disaster. Citing the painters' "crude" use of color, the *New York Times* critic simply asked, "Is this art?" And that was one of the kinder reviews. The American reaction to the upstart Impressionists was so negative, in fact, that the customs office ended up revoking the show's duty-free bond. Of the 289 works on display, only 15 sold—none for more than a few hundred dollars.

As with the Impressionist works of a century ago, the treasures of tomorrow are affordable today—provided you know where and, more important, *how* to look for them. The very rich, seeking to diversify their holdings, have always known that collecting enriches not only the soul but also the pocketbook. A few of us have made bringing the average person into the art and antiques marketplace our top priority, and as you will see in the next chapter, that approach has worked spectacularly. As Auntie Mame said, "Life is a banquet and most poor suckers are starving to death!" I invite you to pull up a chair and join our movable feast.

Games
Auctioneers Play

"Ladies and Gentlemen, We Offer for Your Competition . . ."

The auction held at Sotheby's the evening of November 11, 1987, got off to a routine enough start. I clipped my microphone to my tie, climbed up into the canopied nineteenth-century preacher's pulpit that serves as my auctioneer's podium, checked out the crowd, and got down to work. The hammer came down on one Impressionist masterpiece after another before the small circular stage turned to reveal the real star of the evening: *Irises,* a 28-inch by 37-inch van Gogh painting placed on the block by John Whitney Payson because the painting had grown too valuable to keep. He couldn't insure it and, for tax reasons, he couldn't even afford to give it away.

Before long there was spirited bidding between two collectors on telephones manned by Sotheby's staffers. I felt like a referee at a tennis match as the bid bounced from one phone to the other: "Forty-seven million now. Forty-eight million dollars for it. Forty-nine million dollars now. I have forty-nine million dollars against you in the center. . . .Will you say fifty? At forty-nine million then on the far phone. At forty-nine million then. All done . . . you still there? Fair warning. Sold! For forty-nine million." A roar went up from the audience. The $49 million—$53.9 million with the buyer's premium added—is the highest price ever paid for a work of art anywhere. The whole exhausting, exhilarating, mind-spinning drama took all of three and a half minutes. That's *$14 million a minute*.

The identity of the buyer remained a mystery for over a year, until the Australian billionaire Alan Bond 'fessed up and proudly hung the painting in his fifty-first-floor penthouse office in Perth. There, overlooking the Indian Ocean, van Gogh's *Irises* is being kept company by a Renoir, a Gauguin, a Toulouse-Lautrec, and Bond's personal favorite, Pissarro's *Peasant at Sunset*. It turns out Alan Bond may have been motivated at least in part by patriotism when he bid the record $49 million for *Irises*. "Why should all the great masterpieces," he asked, "be in London or New York or Japan or France?" Why indeed.

Breaking records is as important and, needless to say, as personally gratifying for auctioneers as it is for Olympic track and field stars. And my father shattered more than his share. Louis J. Marion, started out at the age of sixteen in the mail room at the firm that would later become Parke-Bernet (be sure and pronounce the "t") and by 1951 was chief auctioneer. He took me to my first auction when I was about twelve—mainly to get me out of my mother's hair—but whatever the reason for bringing me there, the auction house quickly became a second home for me.

When my dad hammered down Rembrandt's *Aristotle Contemplating the Bust of Homer* in 1961 for $2.3 million—more than twice the previous record for a work of art at auction—I vowed to myself that someday I'd top him. But I certainly didn't count on it taking eighteen years. When Frederic Edwin Church's American masterpiece *Icebergs* was discovered at a home for boys in Manchester, England, I knew I had a tremendous opportunity on my hands. But I was also concerned that the painting, which measures 64 inches by 112 inches, might just be too big to attract many bidders. I needn't have worried. The Texan Lamar Hunt paid $2.75 million for *Icebergs,* and the first call I placed was to my father. He couldn't have been prouder that I was the one to break his record.

Ironically, the record that took eighteen years to smash stood for less than three months. The sale itself, of J. M. W. Turner's spectacular *Juliet and Her Nurse,* turned out to be one of the longest and most nerve-racking in memory. Within moments, bidding narrowed down to an Argentinian collector's agent in the audience and an English collector on the telephone. By increments of $100,000, the bidding climbed gradually until it finally went to the Argentinian for $6.4 million ($7.1 million, including the premium). The poor Englishman on the phone just hung up. All in all, the bidding took a little under seven minutes—an eternity at an auction. But then, when you're spending millions on a painting, you shouldn't be rushed.

As I look back over the fifty-three years our family has been connected with Sotheby's, it seems amazing to me that as a young college graduate I had absolutely no intention of following in my father's footsteps. I was always interested in business and sales, but really wanted to make my own way. Like so many sons, I didn't want to do *just* what my father did. Besides, the whole auction process was much stuffier back then. I was eager to break free and blaze trails of my own.

After earning a bachelor's degree in sociology—yes, sociology—at Fordham University, I enrolled in Navy Officer Candidate School at Newport, Rhode Island. After graduation, I asked to be stationed in either London, Paris, or Rome and was sent to the next-best place: Guam. Once my three and a half years in the

Navy were up, I realized that Parke-Bernet was where I belonged. I needed a job, and the partners there were kind enough to make an opening for me.

In 1960 I started at the bottom of the auction business, literally, taking inventory in the basement at Parke Bernet's old headquarters on Madison Avenue. Sotheby's bought Parke-Bernet four years later; by that time I was general manager. (We were Sotheby Parke-Bernet for more than twenty years—until we decided to drop the Parke-Bernet altogether in 1986. But I am still proud to wear the jade ring my father handed down to me from *his* predecessor, Otto Bernet.)

My first turn at the podium came in 1961, when I was given a small group of books to sell. To get things moving, a sympathetic friend named David Kerschenbaum bought the first lot for $75. I was more nervous about those books than I was about *Irises*.

Chester Dale's Lapel

On November 21, 1961—barely a year after I joined the firm— my father gave me the opportunity to play a part in the auction process. It turned out to be one of the most exciting evenings of my life. Or at least the parts of it I can recall.

That was the evening Dad was to auction off works from the estate of Alfred Erickson, co-founder of the McCann-Erickson advertising agency. Rembrandt's *Aristotle Contemplating the Bust of Homer,* which Erickson had acquired years earlier, was to be the star of the show.

The main room filled up quickly, and two anterooms were added to handle the overflow crowd. My job was to spot bids and relay them to the auctioneer from the doorway connecting the rooms. Since I had had just about enough of taking inventory in the basement, I was anxious for my assignment to go off without a hitch.

GAMES AUCTIONEERS PLAY

I had just started to settle in when Chester Dale strolled into one of the anterooms, walked to the front row, and took a seat directly in front of me. Chester Dale, an impeccably turned-out gentleman then in his sixties, was not only one of the art world's most important and powerful figures—one of the directors of the National Gallery, no less—he was also expected to be one of the evening's principal combatants.

Just before the bidding was to begin, Mr. Dale motioned for me to come closer. "Young man," he said, "I anticipate bidding this evening and when I wish to do so I will signal to you like this." With that, he reached up with his left hand and touched his coat's left lapel. I nodded conspiratorially.

Throughout the evening I kept one eye on the room and one on Chester Dale's left lapel. If a bomb had gone off I'm not sure I would have noticed.

Finally, the big moment arrived. The bidding for the Rembrandt started off at a flat $1 million, which was already more than had ever been paid for a painting at auction, and quickly spiraled skyward from there. Meanwhile, my stare continued to burn a hole into Chester Dale's lapel.

Suddenly, I realized he was motioning to me again. My first thought was that I had been so transfixed that I had missed his signal altogether. But he must have picked up on my apprehension because when I leaned over he smiled and whispered, "Not yet. Watch me later."

Not long after, the bidding for the Rembrandt was over. New York's Metropolitan Museum of Art had acquired this magnificent painting for its collection—and Chester Dale had not touched his lapel even once.

Later, Mr. Dale bought Jean-Honoré Fragonard's *La Liseur* for $875,000. And when he did, he not only tugged exaggeratedly at his lapel, he also said, "Now."

I bring up this story of the Rembrandt and Chester Dale's lapel because I am often asked if people really do use signals— the flick of a finger, the wink of an eye, the touch of a lapel—or if this is merely a fictional device seen in countless movies, just another Hollywood touch.

I would say that 90 percent of auction goers do in fact bid by holding up the numbered paddles that are assigned to them when they register at the front door of the gallery. But there are also those—usually dealers or major private collectors—who prefer to remain anonymous. Often this is born of a desire not to tip one's hand to the competition. Or it may just be that the bidder is publicity shy.

Sometimes these prearranged gestures take the form of a count-me-in-until-I-stop signal. One wealthy Arab gentleman told me he would be bidding so long as the red silk handkerchief in his breast pocket was showing. When the price of one particular item unexpectedly shot up to $55,000, well beyond his limit, he became so excited trying to push his handkerchief out of sight that he actually ripped his jacket pocket right down the front.

Another collector bid by reaching around behind his wife and poking in the back a man two seats down. That fellow, who happened to be wearing a tuxedo, then signaled the bid by taking his glasses off on cue. The auction reached a fever pitch, and the bidder poked the man in the tuxedo so hard the poor guy's glasses fell off.

Norton and Jennifer and Jack and Liz and Dick

The major problem with these signals is that they greatly increase the potential for miscommunication. There is no greater master of this rather Byzantine game than the California industrialist Norton Simon. In his quest for a particularly exquisite Degas pastel, Mr. Simon fooled the competition by having his wife, the Academy Award–winning actress Jennifer Jones, bid spiritedly for the work, then appear to drop out at $1.8 million. Mr. Simon continued to bid secretly with his hand on his chin, and there was this terrifying moment when I wondered if he had just forgotten and was daydreaming. After all, I also had to keep track of a bidder who signaled by holding his pen to his chin and one who was bidding whenever he removed his glasses.

When the bidding was all over, Mr. Simon turned to me, winked—and, thank God, removed his hand from his chin. The Degas was his for $3.7 million. (Later that evening, Jack Nicholson, one of our regular patrons, picked up a Matisse for $430,000. The two-hour Impressionist sale wound up grossing $37 million, another record smasher.)

As far as Norton Simon was concerned, I was very careful to make sure his signal was accurately recognized, because I remembered some difficulty he had had years before. At an auction in London, he gave these written instructions to the poor auctioneer: "When Mr. Simon is sitting down, he is bidding. If he bids openly, he is also bidding. If he sits down again, he is not bidding unless he raises his finger. Having raised his finger, he is bidding until he stands up again." Mr. Simon and the auctioneer got their signals crossed, and the sale had to be temporarily halted. After bidding was reopened, Mr. Simon was victorious and went home with the prize—Rembrandt's *Titus.*

Everyone's nerves were once again put to the test the day Sotheby's auctioned one of the world's great gems, a perfectly cut 69.42-carat diamond. Just before the auction began I was approached by a gentleman from Cartier who said he would be bidding on his company's behalf; in fact, the firm had plans to acquire this unusual stone and name it the "Cartier Diamond." He said he would be standing in the back, near the rear door, and that as long as he had his arms crossed he was still in the bidding.

At that time the record for a gem sold at auction was about $500,000, so as we passed the $750,000 mark the field narrowed down to two—including the gentleman from Cartier. We were going up in $50,000 increments when suddenly it hit me that he may have forgotten his signal! He was standing there so casually, chatting so amiably with several other people, that I became almost totally convinced that he was no longer in the bidding—that the price for the gem was being driven up artificially.

Finally, this diamond was knocked down for $1,050,000 to "the gentleman near the door." I held my breath. To my everlasting relief, he uncrossed his arms and smiled, though he never did look my way or give the slightest hint even then that he was the buyer.

As it turned out, the other bidder had been acting on behalf of Richard Burton, who was crushed that he had lost out. He had intended the magnificent diamond as a gift to his wife. Overnight we negotiated with Cartier on Burton's behalf and helped arrange a private sale. Although christened the "Cartier Diamond," the jewel became better known as the "Elizabeth Taylor Diamond."

Another bidder determined to conceal his identity was Joseph H. Hirshhorn, the industrialist whose enormous collection of contemporary art is now housed at the Smithsonian in the museum that bears his name. After one auction in which he had fared poorly, Hirshhorn approached me in a rage because he thought his cover was blown. From that point on, I called him "Mr. O'Brian," and all purchases made by Hirshhorn or on his behalf went to "The O'Brian Collection." After a time, we became friendly enough for me to kiddingly call him "Uncle Joe." Only a handful of insiders knew that Uncle Joe O'Brian was none other than the legendary Mr. Hirshhorn.

Signals and secret understandings aside, I have conducted so many auctions over the past twenty-seven years—1,300, at last count—that I can tell whether a potential bidder has dollar signs in his eyes or those little X's that mean "I pass." I've also developed a strong sixth sense about who is going to bid and when. Of course it sounds crazy, but I can anticipate when somebody's going to bid. First, I actually *feel* the energy coming from one side of the room. I turn toward the source of energy, and a split second later the person sitting there bids. It seldom fails.

Myths and Misconceptions

Forgive me for making the auction house seem like some sort of rich man's cult, presided over by a gavel-wielding high priest and rife with secret rituals. Unfortunately, that's not far from the prevailing public image. Few institutions are so widely misunderstood—and with good reason. Until the early 1970s, auction houses *were* stuffy places that catered primarily to the Old Money crowd; people in blue jeans were not exactly welcomed with open arms. Is it any wonder, then, that the following comments can still be overheard?

"I have to be rich or at least willing to spend a lot of money."

Of the 200,000-plus lots sold at Sotheby's each year, more than half sell for under $5,000, and *one quarter sell for $1,000 or less.* As the public marketplace, the auction house is the stock exchange of the art and collectibles world, and therein lies its appeal for the small collector: even the novice is more or less on an equal footing alongside the dealers, gallery owners, and museum representatives with years of experience. And although an auction house is a retail operation in the loosest sense of the word, when you acquire something at auction you are, almost by definition, buying at less than "retail"—that is, what you would pay an art gallery or antiques dealer for the same item. Whereas once nine tenths of our customers were professionals—dealers, museums, and the like—now less than half are. The majority are individual collectors like yourself.

This is no accident. It's been obvious for some time that the most effective way to stimulate the art market is to open the doors wide to the general public—to get people to buy, not to intimidate and threaten them. But who in his right mind will show up to bid without at least some notion of what it is going to cost? In years past, every auction house had an attendant who sold catalogues and provided estimates from a list; this person would usually allow only six estimates per customer. Today the estimates for each item up for bid are listed in the catalogues, copies of which are freely available in the exhibition rooms.

"I can't just walk in off the street."

It's amazing that the same people who would not hesitate to walk into a department store and spend $5,000 on bedroom furniture are reluctant to browse through our arcade floor, where estimates for genuine antique pieces often run just a few thousand dollars or less. An auction house is a retail business, there to serve the consumer—albeit the customer in search of a little food for the soul. Walk right in—there are no guards to bar visitors—use the floor directory to find the area that most interests you, and check it out. Remember, the modern auction house is set up so you don't have to talk to anyone if you don't want to. All the information you need will be right at your fingertips.

"If I ask a lot of questions, they'll just laugh."

As I confessed earlier, until relatively recently noses were turned resolutely upward in auction houses, giving rise to our business's image as a sort of flea market for millionaires. Today, auction house staff members are eager to answer any questions you may have, whether you are a potential bidder, a potential seller, someone who wants to have a family heirloom appraised, or you are merely curious. Again, in contrast to the old days, most of our clients are not outrageously wealthy, so there is no need to feel ill at ease. (Besides, there are even ways to buy, sell, or just get your questions answered without ever leaving your home—but we'll save that for later.)

"Auctioneers talk so fast I won't be able to follow what's going on."

Only tobacco and horse auctioneers believe in the Gatling gun approach. Their often indecipherable patter has absolutely nothing to do with the way art and antiques auctions are conducted. Frankly, I've attended several horse auctions and have trouble understanding what's going on. If anything, the art auctioneer's greatest enemy is the audience's boredom. He must be able to get the best price possible for each item on the block while at the same time maintaining a brisk, efficient pace. Since his audience is already well acquainted with the material at hand, there is no need for flowery descriptions or the elaborate sales pitch. Even at the rate of one or two lots per minute, the first-time bidder has plenty of time to keep on top of things.

"If I sneeze or scratch my nose, they'll think I just bid on a Renoir."

Only if you're Norton Simon.

The JLM Theory of the Auction House Appeal

When all the mythology is stripped away, what we are left with is a business that serves as nothing less than the energy center of the art market, a powerful magnet that pulls together the dealers, museums, private collectors, institutions, and the world's most treasured objects in one place at one time. These regularly scheduled sales, which often take us as long as six months to put together, create just the right chemistry of purchasing power in the art world.

This process is uniquely suited to the American personality.

Auctions appeal directly to the competitor in most of us; the daily business of the auction house is by its very nature highly adversarial as individuals are locked in combat for ownership of objects that are valuable by virtue of their high quality and their scarcity. No Super Bowl quarterback was ever more hell-bent on victory than some of the collectors I've seen who were determined to possess that special limited edition print or that one-of-a-kind antique doll.

The auction world is also governed by a strong do-it-yourself mentality. Here a hands-on policy prevails in a hands-on environment. You learn by doing.

Finally, in the world's most consumer-oriented society, it is difficult to think of a business more squarely aimed at serving the customer. Free estimates, free advice from world-class experts, and a guarantee that you will at the very least get what you pay for all make the auction house something of a consumer's paradise.

Do Your Homework

What newcomers to the art and auction world often do not realize is that most of the hard, nitty-gritty work takes place behind the scenes. That goes for the auctioneer as well as the bidder. Most of my time, in fact, is spent consulting with collectors and dealers, carefully examining each item to be sold, determining who is likely to bid and what signals, if any, they may use. Each auction has a character all its own, and it is my job to anticipate what that character is going to be.

Before he or she actually raises that paddle to bid at auction —what I call the final exam—the true collector must go through an extensive process of self-education. For the novice and seasoned collector alike, the curriculum is the same.

Lesson One: Check Out the Auction House's Reputation. Sotheby's, Christie's, Phillips, Doyle, Detroit's Du Mouchelle's. Free-man's of Philadelphia. Skinner of Boston. San Francisco's Butterfield & Butterfield. These and a handful of other houses are the blue-chip names of the auction industry, the firms that set the standard for customer service.

Authenticity and authorship, particularly for items predating the nineteenth century, are not always easy to establish. The difference between the reputable house and the questionable operation is that once the leading scholars in the field have made a determination as to the authenticity of a particular work, the reputable house will stand by its guarantee. Many country barn and sidewalk auctions offer no guarantees at all, and here the buyer had best beware.

Not long ago, I was passing a restaurant in Florida when I heard the siren call of an auctioneer's voice coming from inside. Instantly, my vacation turned into a busman's holiday: I poked my head inside and checked out the action. Somebody held up a tired nineteenth-century landscape while the auctioneer pro-claimed it to be a Vlaminck. He pointed to the signature to prove it. Even from my vantage point at the back of the room it was obvious that this was no Vlaminck, but somebody paid a few hundred dollars for it. I hardly knew what to expect next. A Titian, perhaps. Or maybe a Jan Vermeer painted on velvet?

Sotheby's holds a very valued place in the public trust, and we take this most seriously. Despite the fact that we rarely own what we sell, we stand behind our sales for a five-year period—not just for our commission, but for the whole price. Once we have placed our imprimatur on a sale, we would rather take back an incorrectly described lot and refund the full amount to the buyer than suffer a loss of confidence in the marketplace.

The T'ang horse affair is a case in point. After the writer Leon Harris bought a thousand-year-old T'ang horse at Sotheby's a few years ago, he began to harbor some doubts as to its authenticity and flew it to Boston for testing by the Fogg Museum. The mu-seum determined that it was of a more recent vintage than the

T'ang dynasty, so we agreed to send it to Oxford University to be drilled and subjected to a thermoluminescence test. Oxford concluded that the horse had been unjustly maligned; it was indeed T'ang and Mr. Harris had gotten what he paid for. Not satisfied, Harris had it tested yet again, and again the result cast a shadow of doubt over the poor Chinese steed. The problem soon became apparent. Glazed funeral pottery is often repaired, so certain parts of the horse were more modern than others. We kept drilling the horse's derriere, and Mr. Harris kept drilling somewhere else. Finally, he told me, "I thought I bought a horse, but I really bought a horse's ass." That line alone was worth the price of admission, and we canceled the sale.

Lesson Two: Study the Catalogue. If you do not already subscribe to the catalogues of at least one major auction house (Sotheby's alone publishes nearly three hundred catalogues per year, worldwide), then buy the catalogue for the specific sale you are interested in and scrutinize it. Here the all-important "Conditions of Sale" are outlined, telling the prospective buyer all he needs to know about his rights and the policies governing each sale—guarantees of authenticity, the auction house rules and policies regarding reserves (the minimum acceptable bid), the buyer's premium (10 percent added on to the final bid), and so on.

Once you are fully familiar with these Conditions of Sale, you can move on to the items themselves. Each lot is described as to the age, artist, subject matter, medium, and of course the all-important price estimate. Many lots are illustrated with black-and-white photographs or, in the case of more important items, reproduced in color. All of which eases the pressure on beleaguered catalogue writers like the fellow who, under the pressure of a deadline, wrote the following description of the fiftieth entry in a sale of minor nineteenth-century English landscapes:

> *English School, 19th Century*
> *Another bloody river landscape with a brace*
> *of cows mooching around in the foreground.*

Lesson Three: Check Out the Merchandise. No matter how detailed the catalogue description and illustrations, there is no substitute for the real thing. One of the most common misconceptions is size. Despite the fact that dimensions of each item are clearly listed, people are often surprised to find that the sweeping seascape they so admired is Lilliputian, or that the charming little Art Deco bronze is too big to fit on any table in their house.

Exhibitions are usually held between three and five days prior to every auction. Go, and carefully examine the items that interest you. Browse. Handle things. Auction houses have a wonderful kind of "please touch" policy. Pick up that Ming vase. Sit in the Chippendale chair. Play an old 45 on the vintage Wurlitzer jukebox. Try the cabochon ruby ring on for size. Feel the finish on the Regency console. Handling the property will give you a good sense for what quality "feels" like. After all, at an auction house you have the opportunity to examine objects more closely than at a museum, and to see the worst along with the best.

Lesson Four: Ask the Experts. At Sotheby's alone there are over two hundred specialists in seventy different collecting categories. The names and phone numbers of the experts in charge of a specific sale are listed in the front of every catalogue, and they are available to the public by phone, by mail, or in person—all for the express purpose of sharing their expertise with you and answering any questions you may have. If I buy this painting, should I restore it? If so, who should do the job and how should they do it? Has this piece of Grecian pottery been carbon dated for age? How does this Tiffany lamp compare with the one sold last season? Since the expert wishes to cement a long-term relationship with every collector, he will cater to your specific needs. Many people are surprised when an expert will warn them *not* to bid on an object if that object does not suit the individual collector's requirements.

This is also a good time to double-check the estimate listed in the catalogue with the relevant specialist department. Keep in mind that the estimates listed in the catalogue reflect the prices realized for comparable items at a previous auction—often a sale that occurred months or even years earlier. Quite a lot could have transpired in the interim to either raise or lower the price of that particular lot. When a contemporary painting sold for several times its highest presale estimate at another auction house, figures for an upcoming Sotheby's sale of similar works were hastily revised upward.

So, just to be on the safe side, check with the European porcelain experts in person or by phone a few days before the auction to make sure that the estimate on the beautiful nineteenth-century Wedgwood vase and cover is still between $400 and $600. Ask the Oriental art department if that netsuke figure of a samurai is still expected to fetch in the $750 to $1,000 range. Make one last phone call to confirm that the estimate for the Disney cel from *The Lady and the Tramp* is still $1,200 to $1,500 and holding.

Lesson Five: Attend an Auction Just to Observe. It is essential for any collector to get a good sense of how a particular market is behaving, how competitive the market is—the *feel* of the market. The auction salesroom is, in effect, the collector's most reliable barometer, charting the highs and lows. Merely reading a price list will tell you the final result of the bidding, but it will never reflect the competition, interest, and demand for that particular lot. Actually watching the race run its course is the best way to spot the thoroughbreds, the dark horses, and the nags that finish out of the money.

The Final Exam

The auction house, then, is an open university of art and antiques with a revolving curriculum, a hands-on approach to learning, and a faculty of experts. Now that you have done your homework, you are ready to take the final exam—to attend an auction with the intention of bidding.

Remember that the auction business is seasonal. Virtually no sales are held in late July or in August. The most important auctions are conducted during November and May—a kinetic time for the art and collectibles world. During these hectic fall and spring seasons, Sotheby's conducts two or three auctions per week, most of these beginning at 10:15 A.M. or 2:00 P.M. There are also several major evening sales. Some 75 to 100 lots are usually sold per hour, and you can arrive anytime. My top speed is about 120 lots per hour, but I have slowed all the way down to 40 or 50 items per hour at major Impressionist auctions to give bidders plenty of time to think. It takes a little longer to decide on bidding a million dollars as opposed to a thousand.

Remember that beyond all the solid financial reasons for buying at auction, the point here is to enjoy the experience. There are few things more exciting than an auction. Indeed, I am happy to state that it is the suspense and the drama that keep the true auction aficionado coming back again and again.

Once you've registered at the entrance to the salesroom for your numbered paddle (all you do is give your name, address, and bank reference), you are ready to go up against the most savvy bidders. I have watched countless times as newcomers plucked prizes out from under the noses of unsuspecting dealers and major collectors.

As in any other sophisticated business endeavor, strategy is key. And there are as many bidding strategies as there are bidders. My podium's-eye view of the proceedings over the past twenty-nine years has afforded me the chance to witness firsthand which strategies work best and which are best avoided.

Set a limit. Before you set foot in the auction room, you should have fixed in your mind a maximum figure above which you simply will not bid. Buying on impulse is the single biggest mistake any collector can make. People who spend weeks deciding what stock to buy on Wall Street will pay $500, $1,000, or even $10,000 for a painting or an antique that they are seeing for the first time from fifty feet away, just because it appeals to them —or because they are swept up in the excitement of the bidding itself.

Since it is my job to ignite a little auction fever—to coax, cajole, tease, and if need be shame each bidder to dig just a little deeper into those pockets—you can imagine how difficult it is for me to advise this sort of self-control. Like the stock market or a good game of roulette, an auction can bring out the high roller lurking in all of us. An auction can be considerably more exhilarating than either. Imagine a horse race where bets are still being taken right up to the finish line, or a roulette game where wagers can be made even as the wheel is spinning.

For the first-time bidder whose arm suddenly seems to have a mind of its own, shooting up to bid on a Persian rug or a cuckoo clock he can't afford (and sometimes doesn't even like all that much), this lesson can be a costly one. A successful bid is irrevocable and, for that matter, legally binding. Frenzy is almost always the auctioneer's friend, but rarely the buyer's.

One glaring exception to the you-bid-for-it-you-pay-for-it rule was the distinguished-looking gentleman who swept into Sotheby's a few years ago and proceeded to snap up millions of dollars' worth of paintings. The fellow took bows all evening; he was the undisputed hit of the auction.

It wasn't until the following day that we realized we had a little problem on our hands. The man, we belatedly discovered, was mentally ill. Although his wife was indeed wealthy, he was not. There was no way he could pay. In each case where he had been successful, we awarded the sale to the underbidder. Still, when it came to his taste in art, the fraudulent bidder was anything but crazy. One of his purchases, a Manet, now hangs in the National Gallery in London.

Once, right after I sold him an Edward Hopper for the "bargain" price of $1.2 million, my friend Malcolm Forbes confessed that he had "succumbed" to my "tongue-twisting, arm-twisting charms for an expensively long time." For a member of my profession, this is high praise. Humor (just enough to keep things lively but not cloying), infectious enthusiasm, timing, a feel for people, and a dash of showmanship—all are essential facets of the skilled auctioneer's repertoire.

Under the heading of "Fair Warning," here are some samples of the lines I've used to put bidders at ease—and keep them spending:

"Come on, make it an even one hundred thousand dollars. It'll sound better when you tell your friends."

"But if you buy it, you can hang it any way you want." (When it was pointed out that a rare 1750s wall cupboard hung upside down in the catalogue.)

"I'm sure glad you guys are such good friends." (To two bidders battling for the same Winslow Homer.)

"It's against you, sir, in the back." Or "It's against the lady in the blue dress." (Used to give the last bidder, or underbidder, another chance to raise the ante.)

"So why not?" (When a bidder hesitated to up the bid $10,000 on an early O'Keeffe.)

Beyond the breezy one-liners, the auctioneer tries to establish some sort of personal bond with as many bidders as possible. Eye contact is the best way to convince the bidder that you are in fact rooting for him or her—that you *want* that individual to walk away with the prize. But not even this human touch should sway you, dear bidder, into going above your preset limit.

It does console me somewhat to know that many of you reading this will nod your heads now in agreement, and completely ignore my advice when you attend your next auction.

Know the players. Easier said than done. But it helps to know who the competition is. This is especially true of dealers for at least two important reasons. When you see a dealer pursuing a particular object, you can be assured of its exceptional quality and its value in the market. If you wind up going toe-to-toe with a dealer for a specific lot, you as a private collector have the advantage. A dealer is normally buying a piece so that he can turn around and sell it. So in deciding how high to bid, he has to figure the markup he will need to make a decent profit. As his profit margin dwindles, so will his interest, leaving you to make the winning bid.

To find out as much as you can about the dealers, museum representatives, and even other collectors who might be competing with you, do not be afraid to ask the auction house experts. If they are reluctant to cooperate, then you might make a point of befriending more seasoned auction-goers on the premises. Denizens of the art world also tend to be people watchers, and are often surprisingly eager to share what they know with newcomers.

Watch for the buzzes and the lulls. It is, of course, the world record and the multimillion-dollar sale that get all the press. What surprises me, though, is just how often an item will go for only a small fraction of its true worth or much less than it might have sold for on a different day with a different crowd. Almost every time a "star" lot appears, the vast majority of the people in the audience fail to concentrate on the next object, leaving the field wide open to the few bidders who manage to stay cool and pay attention.

This is no longer true of some categories, such as major old master and Impressionist paintings, where there is for all intents and purposes no such thing as a lull in the action anymore.

On the other hand, not long ago at an auction of American furniture—an area I know something about—there were at least a dozen occasions when even as I was bringing down my gavel I was thinking to myself, "Wow, someone just got a buy on that one."

This may be hard to believe when you consider there may be several hundred bidders in a room and dozens more on the phone. But very often, I have found, you can get a wonderful buy simply because people aren't concentrating.

When the experts put together their catalogues, lots are arranged not in ascending order of value—as many auction new-comers believe—but by a number of other criteria (including logical grouping by artist, period, and type). Since some auctions can last three hours or more, an effort is also made to arrange the lots in peaks and valleys rather than grouping all the major items at the end. This creates a rhythm, a pattern of ebbs and flows that is strategically designed to keep bidders on their toes.

Even so, three hours is a long time. Some of the very best opportunities lie in the valleys when there is an almost palpable lull in the auction room—just past the peaks and before the room has had a chance to settle down. It's a little like the mood at a football game after a big touchdown. During the next kickoff people are not quite paying attention; they are still buzzing about the touchdown.

Right after the recent sale of an early flower painting by Georgia O'Keeffe for $500,000, for example, a lovely Winslow Homer watercolor went for the bargain price of only $18,000. At another auction, the crowd was so enthralled over the sale of a major van Gogh that it was all but impossible to get their attention for the small van Gogh that followed it. A perceptive buyer picked it up for a fraction of its value.

The most striking example of this phenomenon is the diamond necklace on which the famous "Elizabeth Taylor Diamond" hung. It was the very next lot after the diamond itself, and the room was still abuzz from the record sale. The necklace slipped by practically unnoticed for $25,000, one third of what it was worth back then, and perhaps one tenth of what it is worth today.

Make your bids clear. We're not running a mystery tour here. The clearer the bids are to the auctioneer, the less chance there is for error. If you're not trying to conceal your identity, the safest and easiest way to bid is with a numbered paddle. If for some reason you don't have a paddle, then raising your hand will do nicely. For those who have arranged some signal beforehand with the auctioneer—scratching your nose, touching your lapel,

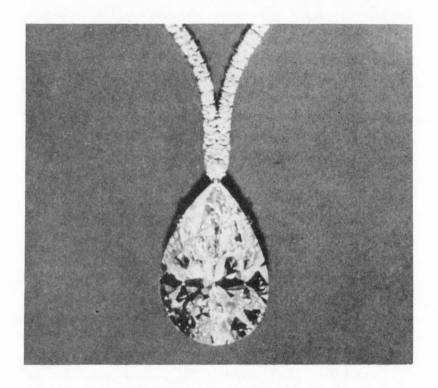

After the Elizabeth Taylor diamond
was sold for $1.05 million,
nobody noticed that the magnificent necklace
it hung from was going for only $25,000.

tugging your earlobe, whatever—be sure and stick with that signal. Any deviation will only cause confusion, something everyone involved wants to avoid at all costs.

How low will they go? Weigh the reserve. As a bidder, keep in mind that nearly all lots are subject to a reserve—the minimum amount for which the consignor (seller) is willing to part with an object. That confidential figure, which is executed by the house on behalf of the seller, is usually fixed just before the sale.

One commonly used formula sets the reserve price at two thirds the median auction estimate. For example, a nineteenth-century needlework sampler with an estimate of $800 to $1,000 would have a median price of $900. The reserve would then be two thirds of the $900, or $600. Accordingly, a Rauschenberg with an estimate of $80,000 to $100,000 would have a reserve in the neighborhood of $60,000, and so on. Again, this formula for setting a reserve is by no means universal. Particularly in the case of very pricey items, the reserve may be considerably higher than two thirds of the median. It is important for prospective bidders to know that the reserve never exceeds the top estimate and rarely is more than the lowest estimate provided.

Read the mood of the moment. It would be wonderful to say that there is a foolproof method for outbidding your competitors on every item at every auction, but no such magic technique exists. The bidder must weigh not only the mood of the auction as a whole but the mood surrounding the sale of a particular lot. Are there a dozen eager participants vying for this prize, or is the audience response decidedly underwhelming? Are dealers bidding against one another, or is most of the action coming from private collectors? Is the auctioneer sweating out the reserve, or did the bidding take off like a Titan missile?

Take all these factors into consideration and tailor your bidding strategy accordingly. It is frequently advisable to come in early because, once a reasonable figure is reached, the auctioneer will often bring down the hammer before your competition has a chance to change his mind and top your bid. On other, less frequent occasions, you might wait until the very last minute to grab the prize from unsuspecting rivals who've been too busy battling one another to notice you. This form of brinkmanship is chancy; the auctioneer may gavel down an item a split second before he spots your frantic wave.

Another, often quite effective ploy is to plunge right in with a high first bid in the hopes of scaring away your rivals. The principal danger here, of course, is that you might have been able to acquire the object for a much lower price. This is a calculated risk, but one sometimes worth taking.

Know when to speak up. We usually open the bidding for an item at one third to one half the minimum estimate. Sometimes it pays for the auctioneer to start things off at an even lower level. Some years ago, I opened bids on a major van Gogh at $250,000. At that level at least five people began to bid immediately, and within forty-five seconds we had passed the $1 million mark. Malcolm Forbes made his final bid of $1,250,000, but an anonymous bidder quickly raised it to $1,300,000 and bought the picture. It's all part of pacing, of firing up that old auction fever. I had a feeling about this painting. I knew it was going to sell well only if I started out at a low figure and allowed things to build naturally. I still remember Malcolm's sad smile of resignation when the other guy got the van Gogh. (Not that Malcolm walked away entirely empty-handed that day; while the big players battled over the major paintings, he managed to pick up a Vlaminck and a small Renoir at very reasonable prices.)

Whatever the opener, things usually proceed from that point on in increments of approximately 10 percent. Bids for an Art Deco armchair with an estimate of $1,000 to $2,000 might start at $500, proceeding in increments of $50 until the $1,000 mark is reached and the increments increase to $100, and so on. Here is where the auctioneer has the discretion to increase the size of the increments to speed things along if there is heavy competition, or reduce the size of the increments to break a deadlock. A deadlock is one of the few times when a vocal bid may be deemed appropriate. If your top bid was $5,000 and the last bid was $5,500, go ahead and say "Fifty-six hundred!" It may just put you over the top.

When You Can't Be There: Executing the Order Bid

Playing the game is half the fun, but if reality dictates that you can't be present in the flesh, placing an absentee bid is a simple and convenient alternative. In fact, almost 40 percent of all lots at Sotheby's are purchased via absentee, or order, bids. Any major auction house will make absentee bid forms available at its offices or in the back of each catalogue. All you do is fill out the bid form and send it in, and the bid department will try to purchase the item you are interested in for as little as possible—usually just 10 percent over the last bid—but not more than the limit you set. If your order bid was $5,000 and your nearest competition bid only $3,000, then you pay only $3,000 plus 10 percent, or $3,300. When an absentee bid is successful, the auctioneer will bring down the hammer with "Sold to the order," and you will be contacted the same day if possible. This service, it is worth pointing out, is free.

An alternative to the order bid is the telephone, and at every major sale there are up to thirty separate hookups directly into the salesroom. As might be expected, many of these calls come from corporate boardrooms around the world. But there are also those publicity-shy bidders who are calling from phone booths in the lobby or from limousines parked outside the auction house. One gentleman was attending a funeral at the Frank E. Campbell Funeral Chapel on Madison Avenue when he sneaked out to bid on a Jasper Johns over the telephone.

More often than not I find myself bouncing among these bidders on the phone as well as several in the audience, but it's

always well worth the effort. An agent for the Italian movie producer Carlo Ponti was furious when the 34.3-carat emerald Ponti
wanted to buy for his wife, Sophia Loren, went instead to the
Annenberg heiress Enid Haupt, who bid from a sweltering phone
booth in downtown Washington, D.C. ("My jewels no longer fit
my life-style," Mrs. Haupt explained when she sold the emerald
five years later for a $120,000 profit.)

Neither of the two highest bidders for *Irises* was in the salesroom at Sotheby's the day of that fateful auction; I was the referee
as they battled via long distance. (The winner's agent was actually
in the building, but bid anonymously by telephone.) The lines
out of Switzerland were really burning up during the Duchess of
Windsor jewelry sale, which Sotheby's conducted in Geneva. I
have this picture indelibly etched in my mind of Elizabeth Taylor
lounging by her Beverly Hills pool, phone in hand, as she suc-
cessfully bid $623,333 for the Duchess's plume-shaped "Prince
of Wales" diamond brooch. Fueled by provenance, the price for
the famous brooch had zoomed to twenty times the presale estimate.

Above all else—and this bears repeating—*do not be intimidated.* We in the auction business are not members of some
secret society, with our own code and our own special hand-
shake. No one is going to throw a net over you the minute you
pass through the front door. We want you to come in and
browse, the way you would at any department store. Keep in
mind that, at least in spirit, every auction house has the same
word flashing over its entrance: Welcome!

CHAPTER — THREE

A

Market

Driven by

Passion

IBM Versus a Statue of Liberty
Weather Vane

At a cocktail party in Houston not long ago, I struck up a conversation with a prosperous-looking wildcatter.

"So," he said, "y'all in the oil business?"

"Yup," I replied. "Paintin's."

Actually, I was afforded my first and only opportunity to conduct a horse auction in Texas. When the bottom fell out of the Arabian horse market in 1988, a bank which had foreclosed on a large ranch contacted us to liquidate the ranch's sizable and formerly valuable herd—the world's largest collection of Egyptian Arabians. Before the horses were sold for glue, the bank decided to take one last stab at selling them at auction.

The evening sale was held indoors in stifling 100-degree heat, yet three hundred people came. There was no reserve, which meant that the prices would have to find their own level. Bidding was unsteady at first, proceeding tenuously at $50 increments, but after five or six horses were sold, a level was established. Three hours and sixty-five horses later, my co-auctioneer Robert Woolley and I were totally drained. But it was worth it, for in one pure auction setting we had reestablished the Arabian horse market, literally overnight.

Someone recently calculated that if the Dow-Jones average had kept pace over the past quarter century with a blue-chip collection of art and antiques, it would now be at about 10,000. I can't confirm that, but I do know that over that same period our business has grown more than 12,000 percent.

While collecting *solely* for investment purposes is never a good idea, to ignore all financial considerations wouldn't be very smart either. How quickly a collection goes up in value is obviously one of the more valid measurements of collecting expertise.

Just how has art stood up against other investments in recent years? In 1981, the Wall Street firm of Salomon Brothers ranked Chinese ceramics as the number one investment area, with United States stamps, gold, silver, and coins rounding out the top five. Stocks and bonds came in fourteenth and fifteenth—dead last. Eight years later, diamonds ranked number one, with an annual appreciation of 24.9 percent. Coins, old master and Impressionist paintings, Chinese ceramics, and gold all remained in the top ten. Once again stocks placed a comparatively dismal fourteenth.

Even the star performers of the stock market lag far behind. More specifically, if you had invested $10,000 in IBM in 1975, the value of that stock fifteen years later (not including dividends) would be roughly $20,000—an increase of 100 percent.

During that same period, smart collectors *tripled* their investments—and better. Had you bought American folk art anytime before 1979, for example, it would have been practically impossible not to make a killing. That was the year of the Stewart E. Gregory sale, which took us all by surprise. Gregory had been the preeminent collector of folk art, but we were totally unprepared for the huge crowd that jammed into our main gallery to bid on his collection. The mob was so thick that I could not squeeze into the room. I had to enter by a side door, pull myself up onto the stage, and climb over the rostrum. People would not leave their seats between the morning and afternoon sessions; they sent friends out to get hamburgers for them rather than risk losing their places.

The Gregory sale was more like a country auction happening right in the middle of Manhattan, and it made history. The whole folk art market was rewritten that day, and the dealers in attendance couldn't wait to get back to their showrooms and mark up their prices. After the sale I called my father, who by then was retired, and asked, "Dad, tell me—what is the most you can imagine any weather vane bringing?"

He knew it had to be a trick question, so he came up with a high estimate. "Four thousand," he guessed, "maybe five, tops."

When I told my father a grasshopper-shaped weather vane had gone for $29,000 that day, his response was entirely predictable. "Son," he said, "you're crazy."

Three years later, a molded, gilt copper Statue of Liberty weather vane brought $82,500. It might command double that if it came back on the market today.

Here are some more specific examples to give you an idea of how the market has performed in the 1980s—a foretaste, I am convinced, of what lies ahead.

• A watercolor and ink on paper by William Murray dated 1806 and entitled *Lipe-Lambert Family Record of Mohawk Valley, New York* sold at Sotheby's in the late 1970s for $2,500. In 1985, the same work sold for $10,450.

The Statue of Liberty weather vane,
in copper, late nineteenth century

• An Etruscan bronze figure of a priestess of Diana, from the second half of the second century B.C., was auctioned on May 22, 1981, for $13,200. It was offered again in 1988 as part of the Stansfeld Collection of Ancient Art. This time the price was $30,800.

• A George III serpentine-fronted mahogany serving table which sold on December 2, 1978, for $2,500 realized a 500 percent appreciation when it sold on April 25, 1987, for $12,100.

• *Play on the Rocks,* a painting by the American artist John Sloan, was valued at no more than $3,000 before the 1980s. By the time it was offered at auction on December 4, 1986, the price was $52,800. This work would probably bring in excess of $75,000 today.

• A Louis XVI ormolu-mounted mahogany *bureau à cylindre* from the last quarter of the eighteenth century sold in the late 1970s for $4,400. A decade later, the same piece was sold for $13,200.

• *Nymph with Laurel Branch,* a painting by the nineteenth-century French artist Adolphe-William Bouguereau, realized a 12,122 percent increase in value when it sold in 1987 for $55,000.

• Sotheby's sold a "Good Parcel Gilt Figural Bronze Mounted Three-Piece Clock Garniture," French, late nineteenth century, for $5,250. Less than five years later, it brought $30,800 at auction.

• In the category of twentieth-century decorative arts, a pair of carved Harewood and American consoles made by T. H. Robsjohn-Gibbings for Peterson Studios in 1937 sold at Sotheby's in New York on December 18, 1980, for $1,540. Less than eight years later, the value had more than doubled, to $3,575.

• John Haberle, a trompe l'oeil ("trick the eye") American painter, painted *Imitation* in 1887. Originally acquired for $170, *Imitation* was offered by Sotheby's in 1987 with a presale estimate of $125,000 to $175,000. The winning bid: $517,000—a 304,018 percent increase, or an average increase of 3,455 percent per year.

There was no greater test of the art market's stability than "Black Monday," the October 19, 1987, stock market crash that saw the Dow-Jones average plunge 508 points—the single worst day in the history of Wall Street. Along with other sectors of the economy, we braced for the shock waves that seemed inevitable.

They never came. Instead of drying up, more capital flowed into the art market than ever before as investors sought a tangible alternative to financial markets. What we saw, in effect, was a post-crash spending spree. Within three days of the crash, a 64.83-carat diamond sold for a record $6.38 million, another diamond brought $3.83 million at auction, and a first edition of the first volume of the Gutenberg Bible sold for $5.39 million. Two weeks later, more records fell at our sale of contemporary art. Prices continued to soar in the months that followed the crash of 1987, as Sotheby's broke the $1.5 billion barrier that season.

The "I Know What I Like" Factor

What is so intriguing about the art and collector's markets is that, no matter how hard you try, you cannot quantify taste. On the one hand, the art market is one of the freest markets in the world, responding principally to the laws of supply and demand. On the other hand, "demand" is based largely on subjective aesthetic criteria.

Certainly this is less true at the higher end of the market. Names such as Cézanne, Frederic Remington, Peter Carl Fabergé, and Antonio Stradivari become, by virtue of their quality and rarity, synonymous with the very best. But as you go farther down the list, where the supply of works by lesser artists and artisans is greater, the more subjective (some might say "fickle") the criteria become.

To give you an idea of just how powerful the "I know what I

like" factor is: Through Sotheby's private client program we recently worked with a major commercial bank to assemble several art packages for investors with large blocks of discretionary funds. The bank had assumed that art as a pure investment was no different from real estate, stocks, or other traditional investments, but the investors themselves had assumed something quite the opposite. They wanted to know who the artists were and what the paintings looked like. They were not about to invest in any art unless it first satisfied their personal taste.

The program was not a success, for art and antiques are the very definition of personal property. They are the tangible expression of one's personal aesthetic sense.

There is only one case I know of where institutional investing in art paid off, and that is the art collection of the British Rail Pension Fund, the major investment fund for retired British rail workers. In the mid-1970s, the fund acquired a wide range of art, from Picassos to medieval brass candlesticks. The collection appreciated handsomely. When the directors of the British Rail Pension Fund sold twenty-five works from the collection in the spring of 1989, they realized a profit of over *$50 million*—ten times their original purchase price. By listening to the experts and not allowing personal preferences to cloud their judgment, those in charge of the fund assembled a brilliant collection that outperformed other investments they could have made.

It's Not Just a Matter of Taste

The rules that govern the art market do in fact differ from those that govern other markets. Art is not a calculated product, like corn flakes or a car. It is created intuitively and responded to subjectively. This all makes the value of a work of art a bit elusive, hard to pin down.

Yet we do not operate in an economic vacuum. Far from it.

THE BEST OF EVERYTHING

The monetary value of something as ephemeral as a Monet or a Grecian urn hinges in part on some of the same external factors that determine the price of pork bellies.

Between 1972 and 1989, the combined aggregate auction sales of the two largest auction houses—Sotheby's and Christie's—increased at an annual compound rate in excess of 17 percent. During this period, there were two declines in those levels—both occurring, not coincidentally, at the height of the major global recessions of 1974 and 1982.

Even in a recession, a lot of prices just keep going up. In 1974 and 1982, Art Nouveau and Art Deco boomed, as did antiquities, Oriental rugs, Japanese art, nineteenth-century European paintings, rare books, antique silver, and vintage photographs. Top-quality objects in all areas are virtually immune to recession. The best of the best will bring top prices whenever it is offered—regardless of prevailing economic conditions.

For the collecting world as a whole, however, volatile world markets have a ripple effect. Riding the crest of the world oil shortage a decade ago, Arab investors used their buying power to buy up everything from major jewels and gold to vintage automobiles and old master paintings. The collapse of the oil market in the 1980s curtailed the Arab influence significantly.

Currency fluctuations and cultural predilections combine to exert a powerful influence on the art market. The strength of the yen against the dollar has made the discriminating Japanese major—often dominant—players in the collecting world, with ample funds to invest in their favorite areas. Japanese interest has centered traditionally on Impressionist and Post-Impressionist art, as well as such nineteenth-century European schools as the Belle Époque and Barbizon. By 1988, the Japanese had widened their scope to include old masters, modern jewelry, Symbolist paintings, German genre scenes, contemporary art, and even Spanish and Scandinavian paintings.

How much money have the Japanese been willing to lavish on their love of rare and beautiful objects? Yasuda Fire and

A MARKET DRIVEN BY PASSION

Marine Insurance, one of the biggest insurance companies in Japan, was revealed to be the buyer of van Gogh's *Sunflowers* for $39.9 million. The 31.26-carat McLean Diamond, the principal piece in the highly publicized 1987 sale of the Duchess of Windsor's jewels, was purchased by the Heiwado Trading Company for $3.5 million, and a Japanese gallery owner set a record for the seventeenth-century Spanish old master Bartolomé Esteban Murillo by paying $1.2 million for *The Virgin and Child* (ten times its presale estimate). During a contemporary auction which followed the Warhol estate sale, a Japanese buyer snapped up a Jackson Pollock for a record $4.84 million, while a Willem de Kooning *Woman* went to Japan for $2.53 million.

Even in those cases where they didn't take home the prize, the Japanese have often driven prices up with their spirited bidding. Nor have they confined themselves solely to big-ticket items. All those world records notwithstanding, the Japanese have also taken advantage of the weakened dollar to purchase American and contemporary art in the moderate range.

So where do bargain-hunting American collectors look to take advantage of a softer currency? North to Canada and south to Latin America, where the strength of the U.S. dollar gives Yankees a decided edge for a change.

The American dollar does not have to compete against the mark or the yen when the item is Americana. While the value of American art and furniture has exploded in recent years, such items have not excited foreign buyers. So far only Americans appear to be interested.

Their loss. Our gain. Unlike antique European furniture that could have been made in any one of a thousand cities and towns, almost all late-eighteenth-century American furniture was produced in seven seaport cities, limiting the supply and enhancing the value. And because Americana is not influenced by the fluctuations of foreign currency, it has enjoyed a slow and steady climb in value over the last twenty years. In 1951, a Goddard-Townsend Chippendale block and shell mahogany kneehole dressing table made in Newport, Rhode Island, circa 1770 sold for $18,000. In 1972, it sold for $120,000 during the sale of the Lansdell Christie collection, and for $275,000 at the history-making Garbisch sale in 1980. Three years later, an identical piece fetched $687,500. Today, the very same Goddard-Townsend Chippendale block and shell mahogany dressing table that sold in 1951 for $18,000 is appraised at over *$2.5 million.*

The same steady rise is true of American paintings. Purchased in 1965 for just $4,750, John Singer Sargent's *Portrait of Mary Turner Austin* brought $60,000 in 1978 and would bring four times that today. Jasper Francis Cropsey's *River Landscape in Autumn* sold at Sotheby's in 1974 for $12,000, and thirteen years later was resold for $45,100—a 21 percent average return per year. We sold Daniel Ridgway Knight's *Woman in the Fields* for just $3,250 in 1966; in 1986, it brought $48,400 (a growth rate of 69.5 percent annually). Knight's *Flower Girls* did even better, climbing 139 percent per annum, from $2,100 in 1965 to $63,250 in 1986.

Edward Hicks, a master of the American naive school, painted sixty versions of *Peaceable Kingdom.* In 1959, one of them brought $8,500; in 1972, the same painting went for $67,000; in 1978, $125,000; and in 1980, nearly $300,000—a thirtyfold increase in twenty-one years.

Even that pales in comparison to the saga of Jasper Johns's vibrant *False Start,* which was shown by the noted gallery owner Leo Castelli in 1960 and sold right after the exhibition to the modern art collectors Robert C. and Ethel Scull for $3,150—half of which went to the artist. On November 10, 1988, the audience at Sotheby's leapt to its feet as I gaveled down the painting for a staggering $17 million. A major victory for American art.

The Global Village Effect

In my opinion, the modern-day boom in paintings can be traced back to a single public auction and public relations bonanza: the sale of Rembrandt's *Aristotle Contemplating the Bust of Homer* to the Metropolitan Museum of Art in 1961. This sale—the first time the magical million-dollar barrier had been broken—fired the world's imagination. Its first Sunday at the Met, more people went to see *Aristotle* than saw the Giants play at Yankee Stadium that day. The art world was no longer a dreary dowager. She was glamorous, exciting, seductive. (Of course, a million dollars isn't what it used to be. At our record-breaking $205 million sale of Impressionist and modern paintings on May 9, 1989, that figure was exceeded no fewer than *forty-four* times.) Incidentally, the number one attraction in New York City today is not the Statue of Liberty or the World Trade Center or the United Nations. It isn't even the Empire State Building. It is the Metropolitan Museum of Art.

Perhaps the single most important factor in the art market explosion is the global village effect—the simple fact that there are more participants in the marketplace, more players in the game. Both people and art move around the globe with far greater ease than they did twenty years ago.

Not that travel is a requirement. Even those who wish to stay right where they are can quickly put their hands on all the information they will need to make an intelligent decision. News of major sales is flashed on television sets and reported on the front pages of newspapers everywhere. Vastly improved modes of communication, from telephones and fax machines to computers, give people all over the world immediate access to the dealers, experts, and auction houses—as well as the means to bid on items being sold in cities thousands of miles away. In short, the Japanese, Europeans, and Americans are all looking at the same works of art at the same time, and they are all capable of acting quickly. Denizens of the musty galleries of old would be shocked to see just how much the art world owes to today's technology.

This "internationalization" of the art world is evident in the tale of the Americans who happen upon a village in the most remote jungle of Central America and begin dickering with the natives for their sculptures. They offer the tribe's chief trinkets and beads. He considers their offer, then disappears into his tent. He returns moments later, thumbing through his well-worn copy of *Sotheby's Catalogue of Pre-Columbian Art.*

Apocryphal? Perhaps. Not long ago my wife and I attended "Indian Market" in Sante Fe, New Mexico, an annual event where five hundred artists and artisans from the region gather to show and sell their wares. By the time we arrived, at 7:30 A.M., it was already too late; thousands of tourists like ourselves jammed the town square.

Finally, we managed to wade through the crowds to a Black-foot Indian selling ornate silver belt buckles. I picked one of these silver buckles, engraved with an eagle, to give to my son as a birthday present. Language was no problem. I just did a lot of pointing and nodding. Then, while I searched my wallet for a credit card, the Blackfoot Indian spotted my Sotheby's business card. "Oh, Sotheby's," he said, almost matter-of-factly. "I attend your auctions in New York all the time. I've bid on some wonderful porcelain there."

Sotheby's has done a little exporting of its own. In 1988, we became the first Western auction house to conduct a sale in the People's Republic of China. That breakthrough event had long seemed inevitable. The Chinese have a centuries-old reverence for beautiful objects and are well aware that there is a huge market for their screens, ceramics, lacquerwork, and jade.

A few months after the Chinese sale, we were treated to a taste of *glasnost.* Sotheby's was allowed to conduct the first international auction to take place in the Soviet Union—a sale of

Russian modern and contemporary artists that earned over $3 million. A bona fide happening, the Moscow auction paved the way for future exchanges between the United States and the Soviet Union.

The global village effect is nowhere more in evidence than at the U.S. auction houses themselves, where collectors and dealers of every conceivable nationality jam our galleries in search of treasures. The fact that people come to Sotheby's from all over the world also means that, regardless of what happens, the show must go on.

When word came that John F. Kennedy had been assassinated, we were in the middle of a sale of German and Continental silver. Maybe we were all just too stunned to realize what had happened, but we pressed on and finished the auction. Years later, a dealer sitting in the front row collapsed with a fatal heart attack in the middle of a sale. I jumped down from the podium, and two doctors in the audience rushed to the gentleman's aid. But there was nothing they could do. After the ambulance came, we resumed the sale. It was terribly hard to continue, but I really had no choice. Many of the bidders had traveled thousands of miles just for this auction, and canceling it would have placed a considerable hardship on them.

JLM's Climate Theory

I believe *what* people collect is determined to a great extent by *where* they live. Belle and Jack Linsky—she brought to this country from Russia by her cousin, the cottage cheese tycoon Sam Breakstone; he the inventor of the stapler and founder of Swingline—were two of the greatest collectors I ever encountered. Their lavish Manhattan residence was brimming with old master paintings, many of which now fill the Jack and Belle Linsky Gallery of the Metropolitan Museum. Not surprisingly, the

Linskys were regulars at both Parke-Bernet and Sotheby's, and I had the pleasure of steering them toward some of their finest acquisitions.

One day, however, Belle told me she was interested in acquiring a painting by Jean Dubuffet. It seemed to me the large modern work would be entirely out of place among the old masters that filled their classically furnished apartment.

"Why on earth," I asked bluntly, "would you be interested in that?"

Well, she was, and she bought the Dubuffet. It was not until they invited me to their sprawling, glass-walled, light-filled Palm Beach home that I realized just how right Belle had been. Here was the Dubuffet, amidst a dazzling array of works by such artists as Picasso, Degas, Franz Kline, and Jackson Pollock. The pieces were perfectly suited to this open, airy Sunbelt setting.

The Linsky's Tale of Two Cities illustrates the way in which art mirrors our surroundings. It also explains why the great collections tend to be in the Northeast, where half an individual's life is spent indoors trying to escape the cold. The heavy oils of the old masters and rich, dark antiques can be warm and comforting in this setting. They seem less appropriate in the warmer climates, where more time is spent outdoors and less on decorating one's "cave." In the West and the South, more emphasis is placed on works that blend with the outdoor life-style and contemporary architecture—Western art, American Indian art, modern and Oriental art, contemporary prints, and so on. Among market forces the climate theory steers collectors toward the objects that blend well with their environment, thus shaping the nature of the market in each region.

Supply and Demand

The art market, like any other market, is governed by the basic laws of supply and demand. There are more bidders than ever before, but only a finite number of objects to be offered. The demand grows, while the supply remains constant or even diminishes—the perfect formula for heated competition.

A graphic (albeit stratospherically expensive) example of how this works is Piet Mondrian's *Composition in a Square with Red Corner,* which Sotheby's sold in 1986 as part of the estate of James Johnson Sweeney, a former director at both the Museum of Modern Art and the Solomon R. Guggenheim Museum. The painting is one of only sixteen known classic diamond-shaped paintings Mondrian created between 1918 and his death in 1944. Sweeney purchased the painting for a modest sum when he visited the artist's studio in 1936. Now one of only two such Mondrians still in private hands, it brought $5,060,000.

People understandably respond most enthusiastically to fresh material. Much of the excitement created by Frederic Church's *Icebergs* can be attributed to the fact that it had vanished for nearly a century. That, in part, is why it sold for $2.75 million in 1979. Had *Icebergs* come back on the market a month later, I doubt if it would have made that price, simply because it would have been made available again too soon. It would have seemed too easy to get. On the other hand, if it came on the market today, it might bring twice the price. But since *Icebergs* has now been donated to a museum, and thus probably taken off the market for good, nobody is likely to get another crack at it.

Although among contemporary artists he has by no means gone unappreciated, Andrew Wyeth managed to ignite a fire storm of controversy in 1986 when he told the world about his Helga collection. The collection of 240 paintings and drawings of his favorite model was bought by one individual, who put them on exhibit at the National Gallery, and within a few months of this announcement, other works by Wyeth climbed 25 percent in value. A top-of-the-line Wyeth tempera brought $600,000 in late 1986, and the same work might command twice that price today.

The United States government has even contributed a fresh supply to the art market. Back in 1984, DEA officials arrested a drug kingpin and seized all his assets—including a wonderful collection of Tiffany lamps, glass, and metalwork. The federal government consigned the entire batch to Sotheby's. The high presale estimate was $1.1 million, but the convicted drug dealer's collection brought over $2 million—enough to buoy the market for Tiffany once again.

On a more down-to-earth level, many everyday items that were once discarded without a second thought now fetch handsome prices indeed: Fiestaware, Mickey Mouse watches, Bakelite radios, baseball cards, comic books—the list is endless.

Sometimes, the supply can change rather suddenly, causing either a drop or a jump in price. When DeBeers Consolidated Mines, which controls 90 percent of the world's rough diamonds, failed to keep a tight rein on supply in the late 1980s, the overflow of gems in the marketplace pushed diamond prices down. By the same token, a doctor with one of the leading collections of Wurlitzer jukeboxes shot himself in the foot by putting too many up for sale at one time. In that case, supply outpaced demand overnight, and prices fell 20 percent.

Trickle-Down

Reaganomics aside, the supply and demand cycle also accounts to a large extent for a trickle-down or domino effect in the art world. By this process, the healthy price achieved at auction for one item can fuel the sale of another. In the autumn of 1986, we sold the Willing-Francis-Fisher-Cadwalader family's "rare and important" Chippendale carved mahogany wing armchair, made in Philadelphia not long before the American Revolution, for $1.1 million. The sale set a new record for American furniture at auction and made headlines everywhere.

Three months later, up popped a Chippendale "hairy-paw foot" wing armchair. Made in the workshop of Thomas Affleck in

A MARKET DRIVEN BY PASSION

1770 and commissioned by the wealthy Philadelphia merchant General John Cadwalader, this hairy-paw foot design was popular in England in the mid-eighteenth century but extremely rare in the American colonies. Today, only two other hairy-paw foot wing armchairs are known to exist. Still, had it not been for the previous $1.1 million sale, I doubt very much if the second chair would have been consigned for sale, much less commanded the $2.75 million that it did.

Ironically, trickle-down can force people to sell the works they have because they simply become too expensive to keep. Just three months after van Gogh's *Sunflowers* sold for a little under $40 million, another of the artist's paintings, *The Bridge at Trinquetaille,* brought $20,200,000. The back-to-back sales pushed insurance premiums on van Gogh's *Irises* out of sight, leading its owner, John Whitney Payson, to the inevitable conclusion that he would have to sell. All this happened in less than a year.

If that seems like a phenomenal chain of events, consider that trickle-down can occur literally overnight. Just one day after Jasper Johns's *White Flag* sold for a record $7 million, I hammered down Johns's *False Start* for a staggering $17 million.

The trickle-down phenomenon is by no means confined to one-of-a-kind pieces of eighteenth-century furniture, nor to those paintings that sell for seven and eight figures. That fine Daum Nancy cameo glass vase you inherited from Aunt Sally and almost threw away may have just doubled in value following the $5,000 price realized by a similar vase at auction. The walnut sideboard you spent $100 on at a tag sale a few years ago may now be worth ten times that amount, thanks to the collector who paid $3,300 for a comparable walnut sideboard in slightly better condition. As for Great-grandma's Tiffany dragonfly lamp, the $20,000 you were offered by a dealer last year just won't do—not since another Tiffany dragonfly lamp was hammered down at Sotheby's for $60,000.

The Three D's

With such a phenomenal and growing demand, three primary sources continually replenish supply: division, divorce, and death. Indeed, over the last two decades, the auction house's participation in these categories—I call them the three D's—has increased tremendously. I'm not suggesting that there are more people dividing their estates, divorcing their spouses, or simply dying today than there were twenty years ago. But more people have come to realize that when they are faced with selling off assets, the auction house provides an expanded range of services geared to the private client, the executor, and the dealer. Where else can you have access to a world-class team of experts who can properly identify, appraise, and ultimately offer your property to an international audience?

Division. Dividing property fairly among business partners or family members can be a very sensitive affair. In many cases, offering the property at auction is the only logical solution. You can divide money. Dividing a Rembrandt is a little more difficult.

Or even a Rembrandt Peale. While he executed hundreds of paintings in his lifetime—most notably his studies of George Washington—Rembrandt Peale's portrait of his brother, *Rubens Peale with a Geranium,* is indisputably regarded as his masterpiece. Painted when the artist was only twenty-three, it combines his talents for both still-life painting and portraiture in one superb oeuvre.

Rubens Peale had been the prize possession of Mrs. Norman B. Woolworth for years. In her late eighties and unable to decide to which of her heirs to leave the painting in her will, she made the difficult decision to sell the picture at Sotheby's and divide the proceeds equitably among her relatives. It was a tremendous moment when I brought down the gavel at $4,070,000—not only for myself and the buyer, J. Carter Brown for the National Gallery, but also for the wise Mrs. Woolworth.

The whole process can take a rather bizarre turn, as when a man acquitted on charges of trying to murder his wife had to find a way to divide the sizable estate with his stepchildren who, to put it mildly, despised him. I wound up gaveling down paintings, furnishings, statuary, and decorative objects worth $11 million. Miraculously, the division of spoils between these warring parties was accomplished without bloodshed.

Sometimes, a collection is split up for the comparatively mundane purpose of raising much-needed capital. Such was the case in 1972, when directors of the Cranbrook Academy of Art in Bloomfield Hills, Michigan, wanted to set up an endowment fund but couldn't raise the cash. So they decided to sell off some of their art works, including Henry Moore's *Reclining Figure,* a six-foot-long elmwood sculpture that sold for $260,000—more than enough to launch Cranbrook's endowment fund.

By way of Monday morning quarterbacking, it's interesting to note that the very same Henry Moore found its way back to Sotheby's a decade later, and this time it sold for $1,265,000. In November of 1988, I brought the hammer down on another Moore *Reclining Figure,* for $2,035,000. And so it goes. . . .

Divorce. The sharp rise in the divorce rate has had, and continues to have, a substantial impact on the art market. Couples unwilling to divide up their assets as part of a divorce settlement often find that auctioning off their possessions and splitting the proceeds is the only solution.

One client of ours became quite adept at this in the course of three divorces. During his third divorce trial, he actually got in the habit of phoning me during court recesses to ask how much objects from his collection were likely to bring at auction. I had to reassure him that, yes indeed, his Fabergé egg was worth $1 million (it actually wound up selling to—who else?—Malcolm Forbes for $1.7 million).

The art world's most spectacular marital dispute was un-doubtedly the twelve-year marathon divorce of the modern art collectors Robert and Ethel Scull. Robert died in 1986, but hostilities did not cease with his death. It was like a United Nations peacekeeping mission trying to get Ethel and lawyers for her ex-husband's estate to agree about anything. But they eventually agreed to let us sell the collection, as long as hers and his had separate catalogues, were advertised separately, exhibited on different floors, and sold on different nights. It was difficult to see how we would determine which paintings would add up to 35 percent of the total—that was to be Ethel's share—and which would total 65 percent for Robert Scull's estate. Yet we forged ahead. Who would get first pick? With the flip of a coin, it was decided that Ethel should go first. As luck would have it, when the sale was over and the smoke had cleared, the proceeds from Ethel Scull's chosen paintings were right on target, amounting to 35 percent of the collection's total worth.

Death. Andy Warhol. The Duchess of Windsor. Clare Boothe Luce. Liberace. As in life, these are the names that make the headlines when their estates are put on the block. But this service is not for celebrities and their heirs only. Historically, the auction house has been the fastest, fairest, and most efficient way to dispose of an estate. Sotheby's has an army of appraisers and administrators who deal on a daily basis with the needs of families and executors. Efficiency is key—Sotheby's has installed a computerized inventory control system, for example—but so is sensitivity.

Naturally, the largest estates are the object of considerable competition among the auction houses. The Havemeyer estate is a case in point. Doris Havemeyer was the daughter-in-law of Henry O. and Louisine Havemeyer, who had given the Metropolitan Museum some of its finest paintings.

Quite a lot of wonderful paintings remained, and when Doris Havemeyer died in 1982, suffice it to say we did everything possible to convince Morgan Guaranty Trust, which represented the estate, that Sotheby's could do the best job. We created a mockup of the lavish Sotheby's catalogue we would publish for the sale, and had our experts do so much research into the Havemeyer collection that by the time we were finished we knew more about it than the surviving Havemeyers did. Even before a decision was made by the estate as to which house would get the plum assignment, we arranged for a top restorer to assess the wear and tear on one of the Havemeyers' Monets.

Still, we had no idea where we stood. Then, without warning, a Morgan Guaranty officer called and made an appointment to see me at 1:00 P.M. My first thought was "Oh, God, they're coming to tell us why they're giving it to Christie's!" I was gazing out the window of my third-floor office on York Avenue when I saw them standing on the street waiting for the light to change so they could cross. The group included the bank officer Gerald Fix, the attorney Richard Kimball, and Doris Havemeyer's son Harry. I asked my secretary what sort of aura they had. By the time they got to my office I was a nervous wreck.

"Have you had lunch yet?" Gerald Fix asked me.

"Yes," I told him, "but I haven't swallowed it."

"Oh, for God's sake," Havemeyer said. "Everything's fine. We want to do business with you."

It was only then that I felt I could both breathe *and* swallow.

The Havemeyer sale brought more than $15 million, and is considered by many to be the auction that, more than any other, launched the rise in art prices that has yet to abate.

As with the Havemeyers, the family of John Sweeney was besieged by offers—including one of $7.5 million for the entire estate. The Sweeneys took a calculated risk when they decided to sell at auction, but their instincts proved sound. The total for the Sweeney sale was $13,785,860.

Most estates, of course, do not include Monets and Mondrians. Yet even if we are talking only about Grandmother's silver service or Uncle Ned's stamp collection, the family is usually more than satisfied with the prices brought at auction. It matters to us, too; sales of estates valued at under $100,000 account for a large percentage of our total business.

From the buyer's perspective, the three D's are a constant source of fresh supply in a business that puts a premium on freshness, since these works have invariably been out of circulation for some time. The three D's also serve as a source of reassurance for the collector: when you know the *reason* behind a sale—that is, division, divorce, or death—then you won't waste precious time and psychic energy fretting about why the consignor is motivated to sell.

The Big Four

The art world may be buffeted by outside economic forces over which it has little control, but its internal dynamics are largely determined by four principal players: the dealer, the auction house, the museum, and the collector/connoisseur.

The Dealer. The art dealers/gallery owners are in the game to make a profit, pure and simple. Toward that end, they act as price supports, arbiters of taste, and tutors to the private collector. "Buy cheap, sell dear" is the dealer's credo, and there is absolutely nothing wrong with that. When the client pays the gallery markup, he or she is actually buying the dealer's expertise and the warranty as to authenticity that goes with it.

The dealer buys at auction for one of two reasons. He is there to replenish his inventory—betting that he will be able to turn around and sell a specific item at a profit—or to bid on behalf of a private collector.

A few dealers have made an indelible mark on the art world. Perhaps the best known of these was Joseph Duveen. The son of a Dutch Jewish art dealer in London, young Duveen bought and sold art at a feverish pace at the turn of the century. He was a flamboyant salesman with an unfailing eye for quality as well as for talent. Duveen hired the legendary Bernard Berenson as his resident expert and by 1914 had virtually cornered the market on old masters. Duveen also had an unfailing knack for locating wealthy patrons.

Duveen moved his base to New York, and from there built the art collections of such titans of commerce as Henry Clay Frick, Henry Huntington, Joseph E. Widener, Samuel H. Kress, William Randolph Hearst, Benjamin Altman, John D. Rockefeller, and Andrew Mellon—all of whom gladly paid top dollar for art works that bore the Duveen stamp of approval. It was Duveen, in fact, who convinced Mellon to endow the National Gallery of Art in Washington and to leave his collection to the gallery. Thanks to Duveen's efforts, more old master paintings are housed in American museums than anywhere else, making these collections the envy of the world.

Duveen was also a pillar of London's Tate Gallery, and added a gallery to the British Museum for the specific purpose of housing the Elgin Marbles. His efforts were rewarded with a knighthood and, in 1933, six years before his death, a seat in the House of Lords.

Duveen set the standard for his profession and established a role for dealers that extends far beyond that of mere salesman. Sack, Wildenstein, Aquavella, and Castelli are just a few of the dealers today whose name can add to the prestige of a work. Of course, not all dealers live up to these shining examples, in some cases charging far more than they should for dubious merchandise. But the majority of dealers are, fortunately for the callow beginner, aware of their responsibility to the buying public. Anyone who has ever seen a dealer inspecting every tiny detail of a painting or antique like some FBI forensics expert realizes just how seriously most of these dedicated professionals take their business.

As the auction houses have grown, there has been some speculation that dealers are being squeezed out of the picture. Whenever I speak to dealers, I simply ask them, "Are you better off today than you were eight years ago?" Not very many can complain.

On the contrary, auction houses and dealers have a symbiotic relationship. As Sotheby's and the other auction houses have opened the world of collecting to a wider public, we have made the dealer's savvy that much more indispensable. Dealers are justifiably proud that they still offer a valuable service to the public.

Nevertheless, collectors who choose to use their services should proceed with caution. There is no test for dealers, and no license. It's up to you to check them out, either through the Art Dealers Association (see the appendix), knowledgeable collectors, or museums.

Are art dealers a dying breed? Far from it. Still, it just might help if they learned to speak Japanese.

The Auction House. Again, the auction house is the stock exchange of the art and collectibles market, and has been at least since the time of the ancient Romans. In fact, after members of the elite Praetorian guard assassinated Emperor Pertinax in A.D. 193, they conducted an auction at which the entire Roman Empire was sold to the highest bidder. (The winner, a wealthy senator named Didius Julianus, lasted just sixty-six days as emperor until he, too, was murdered. Presumably, the empire then passed to the underbidder.)

Sotheby's, the world's oldest auction house, dates back to 1744, when John Sotheby and his partner, Samuel Baker, began selling books to the local trade in London. Our U.S. operation did not get under way until 1883, first as the American Art Gallery and then as the American Art Association. The firm merged with the Anderson Galleries but foundered during the Great Depression. In 1937, two key employees left to launch their own auction house. They were Major Hiram Parke and Otto Bernet.

Parke and Bernet made the perfect team. Members of The

400 felt comfortable in the company of Major Parke (the title was derived from service in the Pennsylvania state militia). The firm's chief auctioneer, he was famous for his patrician bearing, which always lent an air of dignity to the proceedings. Otto Bernet, meanwhile, ran things behind the scenes; he was above all else a no-nonsense businessman who made certain that Parke-Bernet ran with the precision of a timepiece from his native Switzerland. My father, Louis J. Marion, was Otto Bernet's protégé.

London-based Sotheby's acquired Parke-Bernet in 1964, and nineteen years later another link was forged in our Anglo-American partnership when "White Knight" A. Alfred Taubman, a leading businessman and collector, rescued Sotheby's from a hostile takeover attempt.

Today, the business of the auction house is very much conducted out in the open, allowing a little fresh air to circulate through what had traditionally been a rather musty place. There is a famous story about the aged senior partner of Sotheby's making a surprise "inspection" of the immaculate basement storage rooms and complaining grumpily, "Not enough dust! Not enough dust!"

That philosophy, thankfully, is a thing of the past. Whereas once the dealers were the first choice for novice and veteran collectors alike, the auction house of the 1990s offers a depth of expertise, reliable assurances of quality and authenticity, as well as a unique opportunity to examine and even touch works of art and antiques—the very best as well as the worst. It is this variance of quality that is a wonderful teacher for collectors. By comparing objects, one learns what to look for in a work and how to judge its desirability as well as its value.

By pulling the auction business kicking and screaming into the twentieth century, we have assured it of a preeminent role in the twenty-first.

The Museum. This institution is the Keeper of the Flame, a resource center with a twofold mission: to educate the public's eye and maintain scholarship in the arts. By acquiring only the very best items, museums set the standard for quality. Traditionally, they also take the finest objects out of circulation, increasing demand while at the same time reducing supply.

This role is changing, as museums, now operating under tax laws that no longer encourage gifts from collectors to the extent they did in the past, find it increasingly difficult to compete. The booming art market has made borrowing more difficult. When a Giacometti sculpture was lent to the Hirshhorn Museum in Washington, all was fine—until another cast of the sculpture sold for eleven times the value set by the lender. Insurance rates on the Giacometti went through the ceiling, and both museums were forced to foot the bill.

While most people are accustomed to the notion of museum curators in the marketplace searching for treasures to add to their collections, they are less aware of the museum's equally important role as seller. Museums are constantly in the process of reassessing the works on their walls and in their storeroom. Occasionally, a work is put back into circulation—a process called deaccession. It is astounding just how many major works are stashed away in basements and never even shown to the public. These, along with the works on exhibit, have increased tremendously in value. I was visiting the Art Institute of Chicago recently and was drawn to a Cézanne still life. Then I realized that I had just sold one of the Institute's lesser Cézannes for $2.3 million. Museums, in short, are still in a very strong position.

Often, the institution puts a work up for sale simply because the curators have their collective eye on something even more desirable and want to beef up their acquisition fund. Whatever the reasons behind a museum's decision to put a work back into circulation, it's all part of the cycle that replenishes supply and reinvigorates demand.

Museums, of course, don't have to participate directly in the business of buying and selling to stimulate demand. Every time there is a special museum exhibition, the result can be seen almost instantly in the marketplace. Prices for Picasso, van Gogh,

A MARKET DRIVEN BY PASSION

Renoir, O'Keeffe, Degas, and other painters soared after special retrospectives of the artists' works in major museums across the United States and around the world. The touring King Tut exhibition that made headlines in the late 1970s triggered a huge jump in the demand for Egyptian antiquities, just as Diana Vreeland's lavish costume exhibitions at the Metropolitan Museum in New York helped to create a whole new market for antique clothing.

These institutions also wield tremendous grass-roots power in the collecting world. A museum is where the newcomer usually begins his odyssey of discovery—merely wandering about at first, then going to special exhibitions, taking guided tours, attending lectures. It is, in short, where most of us get bitten by the collecting bug. For which, I am happy to say, there is no known cure.

The Collector/Connoisseur. You, the private buyer, are the single most potent force in the art and antiques market today and the reason for the continuing surge in prices. Perhaps you are a knowledgeable connoisseur with the means to indulge your passion for the Impressionists, a new vice president whose assignment is to amass a first-rate corporate art collection, or a young career person trying to liven up the bare walls of your apartment. Maybe you are the family looking for affordable quality antiques to decorate your suburban home or the baby boomer wanting to hedge your bets by investing at least 10 percent of your assets in something tangible. Whatever your particular situation and whatever your specific motives, you have forced the museums, the dealers, and the auction houses to cater to your needs and anticipate what will interest you.

A Glimpse into the Future

I don't have a crystal ball, and neither does anyone else in the business. There is no way to predict what will happen five years from now. But I do have a pretty good idea of what is going to happen a few months down the road. If people come to me with a specific question regarding an area of collecting, I can tell them that now is the time to buy or sell, or that perhaps they should wait awhile for market conditions to improve. Whatever the advice, it is predicated on an ability to see a few months into the future, and no further.

For a longer view, Sotheby's charted the prices in all major collecting areas for *Forbes* magazine, and looking at these will at least give you a sense of trends which show where specific markets have been and seem to be heading.

Platinum Opportunities

What surprises most newcomers to the art and auction scene is not the astronomical sums that some people are willing (and able) to pay, but the extraordinary buys that are still available—a signed Picasso print, limited edition of 300, for $1,760; an 18-karat gold open-faced Patek Philippe watch, circa 1890, for $1,870; a three thousand-year-old Egyptian bronze statue for just $935.

Remember, nearly one quarter of the 200,000 lots we auction at Sotheby's each year sell for *less than $1,000*. For the aspiring collector with some discretionary income at his or her disposal, opportunities positively abound in today's art and antiques market, not only at the auction houses but at dealers' galleries and antiques shops as well. Believe it or not, there are still a few Impressionists within reach. Camille Pissarro, who occupies a

American Furniture

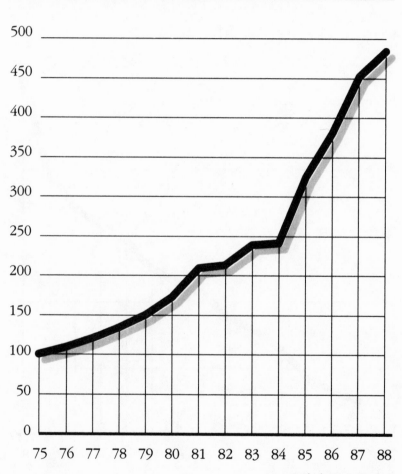

Sotheby's Art Index
Basis: 1975 - 100 ($)
© Sotheby's 1989

American Paintings

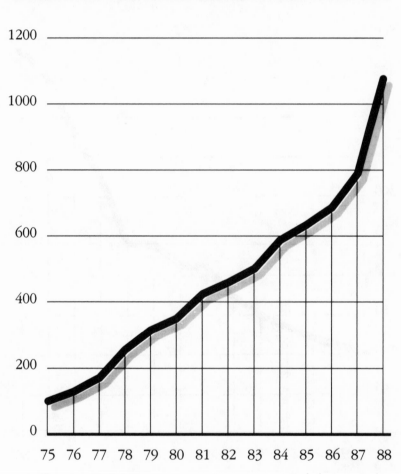

Sotheby's Art Index
Basis: 1975 - 100 ($)
© Sotheby's 1989

Chinese Ceramics

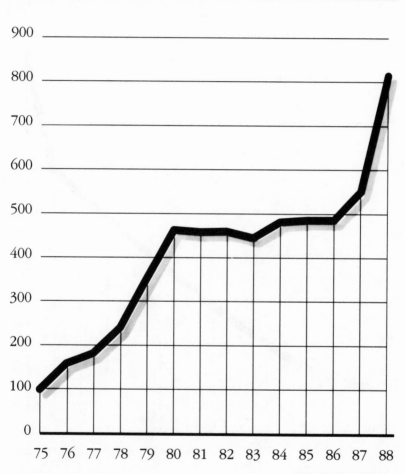

Sotheby's Art Index
Basis: 1975 - 100 ($)
© Sotheby's 1989

Contemporary Art

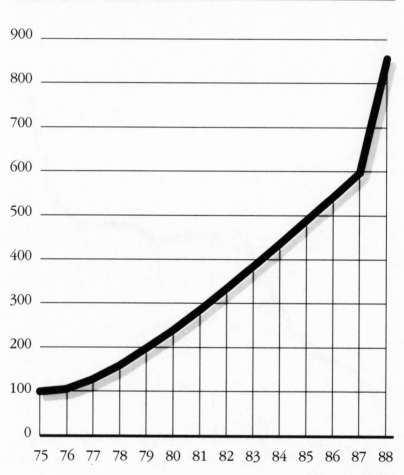

Sotheby's Art Index
Basis: 1975 - 100 ($)
© Sotheby's 1989

Continental Ceramics

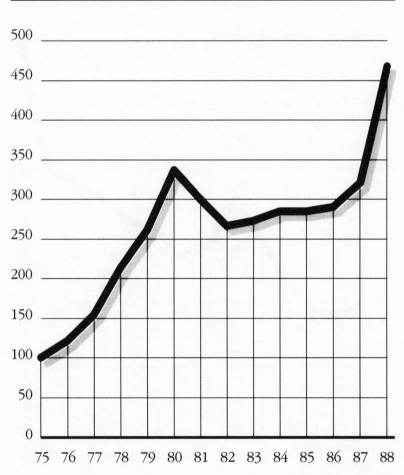

Sotheby's Art Index
Basis: 1975 - 100 ($)
© Sotheby's 1989

Continental Silver

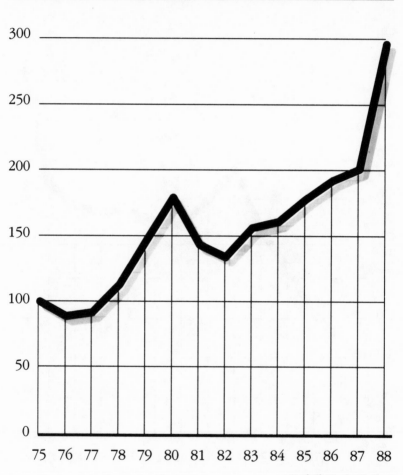

Sotheby's Art Index
Basis: 1975 - 100 ($)
© Sotheby's 1989

English Furniture

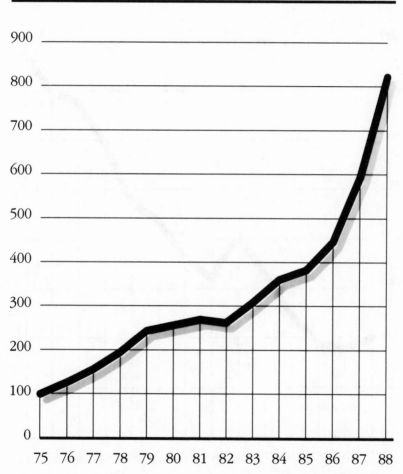

Sotheby's Art Index
Basis: 1975 - 100 ($)
© Sotheby's 1989

English Silver

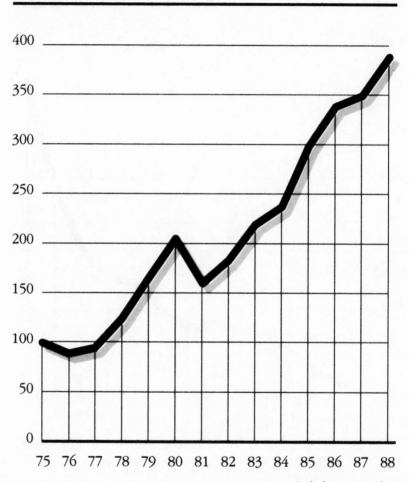

Sotheby's Art Index
Basis: 1975 - 100 ($)
© Sotheby's 1989

French & Continental Furniture

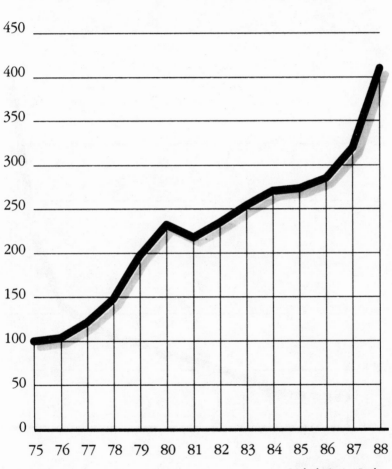

Sotheby's Art Index
Basis: 1975 - 100 ($)
© Sotheby's 1989

Impressionist Art

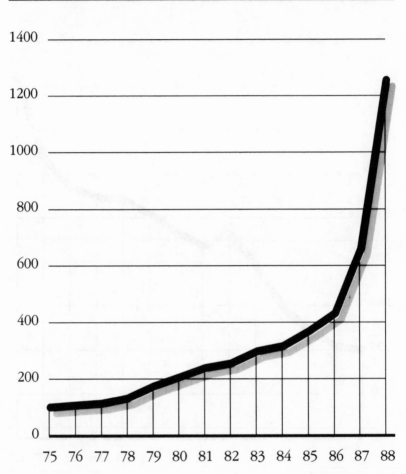

Sotheby's Art Index
Basis: 1975 - 100 ($)
© Sotheby's 1989

Modern Paintings

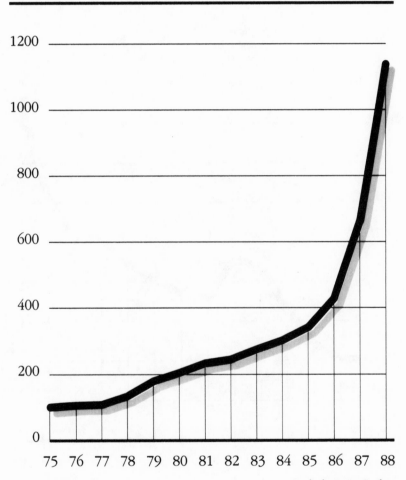

75 76 77 78 79 80 81 82 83 84 85 86 87 88

Sotheby's Art Index
Basis: 1975 - 100 ($)
© Sotheby's 1989

19th-Century European Paintings

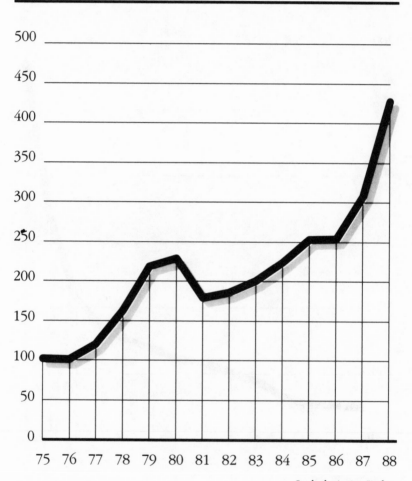

Sotheby's Art Index
Basis: 1975 - 100 ($)
© Sotheby's 1989

Old Master Paintings

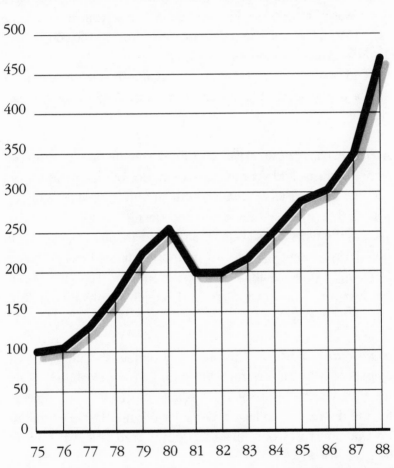

Sotheby's Art Index
Basis: 1975 - 100 ($)
© Sotheby's 1989

spot in the second tier, might command a bit less than six figures. There are even some minor old masters to be had. The art critic Richard H. Rush bought a painting by the seventeenth-century Dutch artist Jan Baptist Weenix in the late 1960s for $1,000, and he sold it twenty years later for $80,000. But as recently as 1987, a fine example of Hubert Robert's work, *An Extensive River Landscape with Figures by the Ruins of a Monument,* signed, circa 1760, was purchased for just $15,000. A Picasso drawing from the late 1950s can still be purchased for under $50,000, and a Thomas Gainsborough for even less.

Old masters aside, the kinds of bargains most of us search for are of the ground-floor variety. Here are some of today's best bets.

African Art. African masks had a great influence on the Post-Impressionists, and yet the finest examples of African art—from carvings and masks to jewelry—are still, in my opinion, underpriced. The more sophisticated and detailed works from areas such as the Ivory Coast, Gabon, and Zaire are already growing in popularity among collectors. The more crudely finished pieces from Upper Volta, Mali, Sudan, Cameroon, and Togo have yet to be discovered in a major way and remain highly affordable to the average collector.

American Furniture. This area is booming, and the finest examples of colonial furniture will soon be out of sight for all but the very wealthy. But some affordable pieces are still available for the discerning collector. Consider the fine 1805 Federal satinwood and rosewood inlaid mahogany card table we sold not long ago for $12,650.

In 1961, I bought a late-eighteenth-century English mahogany secretary/bookcase for $225. Today, it is worth about $8,000. An even wiser purchase for me was a Federal bookcase for which I paid $5,250 in 1975. The bookcase, built by William Appleton of Salem, Massachusetts, about 1810, would bring in the neighborhood of $50,000 in today's market.

*This Kongo Male Fetish Figure, purchased
in 1989 for $1,210, will appreciate
in value as more and more serious collectors
discover African art.*

THE BEST OF EVERYTHING

If Federal furniture is a little out of your price range, U.S. Centennial furniture, replicas of colonial pieces made specifically as part of the celebration of our one hundredth anniversary in 1876, are a wise alternative. These prices will never appreciate as much as their colonial counterparts, but they should enjoy moderate gains while providing a lifetime of enjoyment. A colonial highboy may sell for upward of $100,000 today, but its Centennial replica can still be acquired for between $2,000 and $5,000.

American Paintings. You can't touch a French Impressionist for $20,000, but even less will buy you a fine example from the American school. A case in point is *The Little Bathing Beach, Wisconsin,* painted in 1902 by the very important but still little-known American artist George Oberteuffer. This oil on canvas, which had been exhibited at the Pennsylvania Academy of Fine Arts and the Art Institute of Chicago, was purchased not long ago for $19,800. Another of the many American artists whose work will almost certainly command high prices in the future is Robert Spear Dunning, whose 1902 *Still Life with Peaches and Grapes* was picked up in 1987 for $13,200.

We have already received strong signals as to where this particular market is heading. The most paid for a work by the American modernist Joseph Stella was $16,000, until 1986, when a 1919 painting of Stella's went for $2.2 million.

American paintings, incidentally, can stand up to the best European works. Among the paintings that hang in my home is a serene landscape, and when I ask people to name the locale of the picture they always guess Belgium or France. I get great satisfaction in telling them that the painting is American, and that the bucolic scene is of New Jersey, somewhere near Newark, at the turn of the century.

American Samplers. These small-scale needlework samplers, hand stitched by young girls in the eighteenth and nineteenth centuries, really took off with the sale of the collection belonging

*An excellent
example of American
furniture, this nineteenth-century
pine blanket chest sold
for $2,310.*

*This Federal satinwood
and rosewood inlaid mahogany
card table was a superb investment
at $12,650.*

to the Philadelphia businessman Theodore H. Kapnek in 1981. Within a few years, some of the finest examples were fetching six figures. In 1987, for example, a sampler made by eleven-year-old Eliza Waterman of Providence, Rhode Island, in 1788 brought $192,000. Here are the poignant words little Eliza stitched on the linen square:

> May spotless innocence and truth,
> My every action guide,
> And guard my unexperienced youth,
> From arrogance and pride.

Little did Eliza know.

Some first-rate examples of this uniquely American art form can still be had for a few thousand dollars. But not for long. In addition to its inherent charm, each sampler serves not only as a work of art but as a sort of historical document. As the popularity of samplers continues to surge ahead in the coming years, so will the prices.

Antiquities. A piece of sculpture created thousands of years ago costs a small fraction of the price for a modern Henry Moore. Yet this may not be the case for long. In December of 1988, we sold a three-thousand-year-old Cycladic marble head of a goddess for $2,090,000. At the same auction, a Sumerian white marble cylinder seal circa 2600 B.C. brought $25,300—eight times the previous record set for a similar seal. These sales signaled the entry into the market of collectors and dealers accustomed to paying seven figures for Impressionist and contemporary works—and not afraid to do the same for the rarest antiquities. As prices for these objects go up, a momentum builds that will certainly raise prices down the line. This is, in essence, a tide that lifts all boats.

Although antiquities will almost certainly command higher prices in the future, there is time for the smaller collector to get in on the action and share in the wonder of owning a piece of

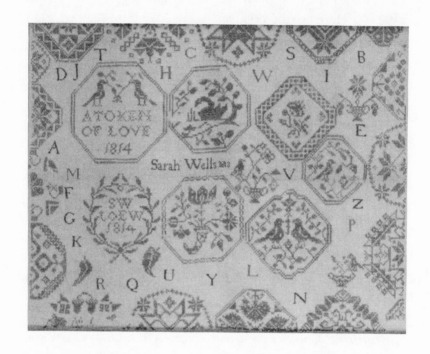

A rare Quaker
sampler purchased for
$1,980 in 1989

*Antiquities like this
second-century Roman marble head
of Pan, which sold for
$3,575 in 1987, are still
quite affordable.*

*This Attic red
hydria (jug) from 450 B.C.
sold in 1987 for $12,100.*

history—whether it be an Attic red-figure hydria (jug), like the one sold in 1987 for $12,100, or a three-thousand-year-old Egyptian bronze ($935).

Art Moderne Furniture of the 1940s. It took a while for Art Nouveau and Art Deco furniture to catch up with decorative items from these periods. Now that the styles do command top prices, Art Moderne pieces—the streamlined and still very affordable designs of the 1930s and 1940s—are beginning to find a market. This is the distinctive Jean Harlow style of American furniture. Hollywood chic. Oversized, lots of white, very dramatic —the kind Fred Astaire and Ginger Rogers danced around in all those musicals. Fortunately, there are a lot of high-quality Art Moderne pieces around that can be had for just hundreds of dollars, certainly below $2,000. The emerging star of this period is a designer named T. H. Robsjohn-Gibbings, so if this is a style that interests you, Robsjohn-Gibbings is the man to collect.

Autographs. A few years ago I bought a bid slip from a November 18, 1936, auction for $55. The slip was for a group of children's books, and on the back it is signed "Franklin D. Roosevelt, the White House."

It seems to me that the autograph market is rapidly expanding as more and more collectors have become interested in this fascinating subject. The value of an autograph hinges on a number of factors. Signatures alone (S) are less in demand than typed letters that are signed (LS). Autograph letters that are signed (ALS) and documents signed (DS) tend to bring the highest prices, though of course much depends on the signer, the rarity of the signature, the historical importance of the document, and so on. While William Henry Harrison's signature alone can be acquired for about $250, a handwritten letter from Harrison, who died of pneumonia barely a month after his inauguration, was sold at auction recently for $396,000. For obvious reasons, Greta Garbo's signature would now be worth in the neighborhood of

*Pair of 1937 carved walnut
consoles by T. H. Robsjohn-Gibbings,
a master of Art Moderne. They
sold in November 1988 for $3,575.*

*These elaborate walnut
side tables, also the work
of Robsjohn-Gibbings,
brought $2,475.*

$1,000. For the same price, you might also acquire a baseball signed by Babe Ruth. As the five hundredth anniversary of Columbus's discovery of America approaches, a document bearing the signatures of King Ferdinand and Queen Isabella of Spain, which normally runs about $5,000, will almost certainly enjoy a dramatic increase in value.

The autographs of many famous people can still be had for under $100, and some truly historic documents for a few thousand dollars. Malcolm Forbes has certainly been a force to be reckoned with in this field. In addition to Paul Revere's expense account, which set the record for a handwritten American document, his collection includes a series of telegrams sent by Czar Nicholas II's family just prior to the onset of the Russian Revolution. The continued participation of Forbes and other devoted collectors assures that prices for historic documents of this type will increase.

Classic Automobiles. During 1988, average prices for collectible cars accelerated by 30 percent—a result, in part, of sudden interest by Japanese collectors. According to David Brownell, editor of *Hemmings Motor News,* the bible of car collectors, "Anyone who bought a collectible car over the past fifteen years found it to be a pretty good investment." Fifties models are probably your best bet, since the market is well established. Today, the classic 1955 two-seater Thunderbird with portholes may fetch over $30,000; a 1959 Cadillac El Dorado convertible, $75,000. The collector wise enough to purchase a mint-condition 1950s Ferrari for about $25,000 just a few years ago could sell the same vehicle today for $125,000.

Take heart. More than seventy-five American autos from the mid-1940s through the mid-1960s have been designated as "Milestone" cars, and many of these can still be found for under $10,000.

A word of caution: Collecting classic cars is a risky and often expensive undertaking. No matter how well maintained it may have been over the years, a vintage automobile can easily wind up costing $10,000 or more to restore. For many, however, doing it yourself is half the fun.

Collectibles. In a few short years nostalgia has become a powerful factor in the collecting world. Antique dolls range in price from $100 to $100,000 (for a seventeenth-century doll with the original clothing), and the market for them is growing. Walt Disney animated art increases an average of 25 percent annually. The sky seems to be the limit for some articles of movie memorabilia. Dorothy's ruby slippers from *The Wizard of Oz* brought $165,000 at auction not long ago, and more recently we sold the Wicked Witch's hat worn by Margaret Hamilton in the film for $50,000 (the same evening we also sold Clark Gable's annotated script from *Gone With the Wind* for $77,000 and one of the two upright pianos played in *Casablanca* for $140,000.)

The market for collectibles is growing so rapidly that Sotheby's schedules regular "Collectors' Carousels," featuring dollhouses, toy soldiers, games, Bakelite radios, Wurlitzer jukeboxes, circus art, slot machines, rock-and-roll memorabilia—in short, any piece of yesterday that is treasured by others like yourself today.

Early English Oak Furniture. After years of being considered too heavy, dark, and, well, clumsy for a modern home, sixteenth- and seventeenth-century English oak furniture has made a comeback. Collectors of these solid, richly carved (if not all that comfortable) chairs, as well as chests, cupboards, and dining tables might pay upward of $50,000 for the rarest and most sought-after pieces. Yet it remains an undervalued area, with pieces three hundred years or older going for $1,000 or less.

English Salt-Glazed Stoneware. Over the past five years, Amerian collectors have awakened in increasing numbers to the charms of English pottery of the seventeenth and eighteenth

*The dress Marilyn Monroe
wore in* Bus Stop, *much coveted by collectors
of movie memorabilia*

centuries. These attractive collectibles can be as simple as an unadorned jug in blue or brown wash. Or they can be elaborately cast or molded in the shape of houses, shells, animals, or people. While a very rare six-and-a-half-inch-high salt-glazed model circa 1745 of two men sitting in a church pew brought an eye-popping $112,200 at Sotheby's in 1987, many fine examples are still available for under $1,000. As American collectors increasingly see English stoneware as an attractive and affordable alternative to more expensive ceramics, competition will become more intense.

Glass. In the fall of 1987, a woman came in to us with a Lalique green scarab piece that she had purchased several years earlier for a few hundred dollars and which we estimated would sell for about $6,000. It brought $49,000. In fact, Lalique, Daum, and Steuben remain terribly underpriced. Even Tiffany glass is undervalued. While you can pay upward of $100,000 for Tiffany glass, wonderful examples can still be found for $500. But hurry. Japanese buyers are beginning to cast a covetous eye in this direction, and the strength of the yen against the dollar means they will be in the more advantageous position. Higher prices are sure to follow.

Jewelry. Although the Duchess of Windsor's jewels and the egg-sized 86-carat flawless diamond I hammered down in 1988 for $9.13 million grabbed the headlines, you don't have to be Elizabeth Taylor to afford fine-quality jewelry. Auction houses sell wonderful period pieces, particularly Art Nouveau and Art Deco designs, at anywhere from $500 to $10,000—a fraction of the cost charged by retailers. Example: A pair of antique gold cuff bracelets bought at auction only a couple of years ago for $5,000 proved to be a dazzling investment when they brought $125,000 in 1988. There are similar pieces still underpriced; it's only a matter of time before they, too, skyrocket in price.

Another client came to us with an Art Deco diamond, ruby, and emerald bracelet that he had purchased in the early 1980s

*This Tiffany
Favrile glass vase, circa 1896,
could still be had in the
1980s for $3,520.*

Classic Art Nouveau:
a Lalique bottle and
stopper adorned with a dozen figures;
price at auction: $2,200

for about $10,000. Our estimate in 1988: $60,000 to $80,000. The bracelet was sold that year for $445,000. Similarly, a cultured pearl necklace (yes, *cultured* pearls) worth no more than $50,000 a decade ago sold in 1988 for $1.265 million—more than twice our top estimate.

Jewelry from the 1940s in particular is making a spectacular comeback. When women pitched in for the war effort, taking defense plant jobs and joining the military, their wardrobe changed dramatically. The long, fluid clothes of the 1930s were replaced by tailored suits with shoulder pads, shorter skirts, and trousers à la Dietrich and Hepburn.

Wartime brought a change in jewelry, too. Pieces became larger, bolder, more dramatic. Some had a patriotic motif—pins shaped like battleships and flags, bracelets designed to evoke tank treads, and so on. Gold was rationed; platinum production was controlled, and hostilities halted the supply of precious gems from the Orient. So women turned to wearing huge semi-precious stones: amethysts and aquamarines and peridot and beryls the size of walnuts and Ping-Pong balls.

When the war ended in 1945, women shed their uniforms and work attire and embraced a new, softer image. Their forceful forties jewelry, no longer appropriate, was relegated to the back of the dresser drawer. After more than forty years of being considered unstylish, even crass, forties jewelry is coming back in style with a vengeance. If you don't have an example of your own around the house somewhere—perhaps a flashy bauble Grandma used to wear—some remarkable pieces can be obtained for only several thousand or even a few hundred dollars.

It bears repeating that, regardless of its investment potential, jewelry bought at auction is invariably a bargain—particularly if it is signed by the designer. For example: A magnificent pair of cabochon sapphire and diamond ear clips by David Webb purchased at Sotheby's not long ago for $8,525 could also be seen in the window of one Fifth Avenue store. The retail price was $20,000.

A gold and
diamond Cartier brooch
circa 1940;
price at auction: $1,760

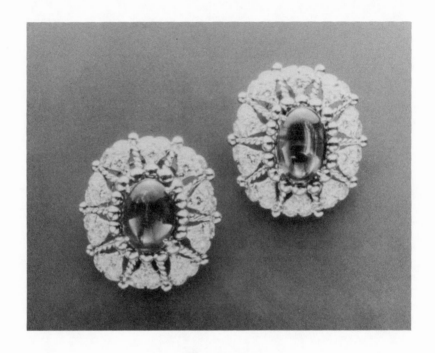

*This signed pair
of sapphire and diamond
earclips by David Webb
was acquired at auction
for $8,525; retail price:
more than $20,000.*

Latin American Art. With a few exceptions (Diego Rivera, whose work can cost $400,000 or more, being the most obvious), the Latin American painters have yet to be discovered. There are hard monetary reasons for this. The economies of most Latin American countries are in deep trouble, and their currencies are severely depressed. So, dollar for dollar, most works even by superb Latin American artists can be purchased at very attractive prices. This is one of the few areas where the novice collector can get in on the ground floor today.

Mission Furniture. This has been one of the hottest items in California and the American Southwest for the past decade. Mission oak furniture, which comes under the heading of arts and crafts, is relatively inexpensive right now; most pieces can still be purchased for under $1,000. But the supply is so limited that its value is bound to increase dramatically.

Modern Drawings. First-rate works by even the greatest modern artists remain well within reach. A perfect example is Alexander Calder's *Two Heads*. A drawing in gouache and India ink on paper, *Two Heads* is signed and dated 1971. Recent auction price: $4,400.

Nineteenth-Century Caucasian Rugs. The brilliant hues and bold geometric designs of the carpets woven in the valleys of the Caucasus have made them a relatively new favorite among collectors. While the most sought-after rug might bring in excess of $20,000 at auction, most Caucasian carpets can still be purchased at a significantly lower price. A beautiful indigo and rose 9-foot 2-inch by 6-foot 3-inch Shirvan carpet was sold recently for only $2,899. At about the same time, a pair of Mashhad Tree of Life rugs was purchased for $1,078, and a magnificent beige Kerman meditation carpet for only $1,056.

The same holds true for all varieties of Oriental rugs and carpets. For well under $5,000, the most spectacular Chinese and

Alexander Calder's
Two Heads

Persian rugs can be acquired at auction. These carpets are not only less expensive than most wall-to-wall or machine-made rugs, they will appreciate in value over the years. In the meantime, you can take pleasure in walking barefoot on a century-old work of art.

Nineteenth-Century European Bronzes. Some wonderful sculptures, particularly French nudes, can be bought for a few thousand or sometimes even a few hundred dollars. Two examples: Eugène Marioton's bronze figure of a lion tamer, circa 1880, which was acquired for just $431 in 1987, and Hippolyte Moreau's bronze figure of a woman representing Sunset, which went for under $2,000. This is an area where the supply is still plentiful, and therefore a good place for new collectors to look.

Prints. Currier & Ives prints and prints of works by other American artists, such as Whistler and Winslow Homer, are superb things to buy. So, too, are European prints. An 1863 etching of Jean-François Millet's famous *Le Départ pour le travail* was sold not long ago for only $4,950—in my opinion, a tremendous value. If your taste runs to the modern, a top-quality limited edition Picasso print signed by the artist can still be had for under $2,000, while other Picasso prints can be worth hundreds of thousands of dollars. But beware. There are many dubious works out there, such as framed pages from illustrated books or photomechanical reproductions. Be careful where you buy such works.

Silver. A fine collection of Georgian silver can be assembled for a moderate sum. Storr and De Lamerie are two makers whose mark will always bring top dollar, but you can find terrific bargains among the less renowned English and Continental silversmiths.

Opportunities also abound in the area of American silver. Bringing their European tastes with them to the New World,

European bronzes remain
affordable, such as this
nineteenth-century French figure
which sold not long
ago for $3,025.

A tremendous value:
a fine print of Jean Francois Millet's
famous Le Départ pour le travail,
purchased in the late 1980s
for $4,950

the early colonists nonetheless eschewed the trappings of aristocracy. Their silver teapots, mugs, porringers, and bowls are simple, functional, and, in comparison to the Early American furniture that they once sat on, highly affordable.

Collectors of silver pay close attention to condition—ideally, no repairs or splits, a clear maker's mark, and original engraving. There are a few superstars among eighteenth-century silversmiths, including Simeon Soumaine, John Coney, Joseph Richardson, and Myer Myers, who owes some of his current appeal to the fact that he was Jewish and would probably have been discriminated against in Europe but was able to flourish in New York. Another well-known silversmith whose work fetches higher prices is Philip Syng, Jr., who made the inkstand used for the signing of the Declaration of Independence. Of course, no silversmith's work is more highly prized than that of Paul Revere. Even a pair of simple sugar tongs will go up fifty times in value if it is clearly marked as Revere's handiwork.

If we leap ahead a couple of centuries, we can see that early designs by Gorham and Kirk are available to the astute collector at affordable prices. Amazingly, even a Tiffany silver tea set, circa 1920, can still be had for $1,500—one sixth the retail price of a Tiffany tea set manufactured last week! The whole array of nineteenth-century American silver—from water pitchers and candlesticks to tea sets, vases, and goblets—can be purchased at auction for similarly low prices. Perhaps the greatest value is flatware. Sotheby's recently sold a 1915 service for twelve of Georg Jensen flatware for $3,750. The same Georg Jensen pattern manufactured today sells for $11,280 retail—and that is just for a single five-piece place setting!

Western and Native American Art. With the decline of the oil business in the 1980s, prices have fallen dramatically for fine-quality Western paintings and bronzes and for such American Indian art objects as Navaho rugs, Pueblo pots, Zuñi ceremonial jars, Apache baskets, and Hopi kachina dolls. It is practically im-

An 1809 American silver tea set;
price at auction: $2,970

possible to find anything that's gone down in the last few years, so this area represents a tremendous opportunity for those growing numbers of collectors who find the art of the American West fascinating.

There is no foolproof way of predicting how a particular area will perform. But opportunities abound for the collector who is willing to do his homework. Whatever the dynamics of the art market at the particular time you decide to jump in, you must ultimately be guided not by trends but by your heart—and your head.

Ropin' the Stallion,
purchased at auction in 1988
for $1,650

*In 1988 a Western art collector
paid $5,500 for two bronzes
by Curtis Fort, including*
The Barrel Racer.

CHAPTER — FOUR

How To

Assess Value:

Nine Denominators

You are ready to begin collecting. But what do you look for in a work of art? What are the guidelines to consider? If the following "Nine Denominators of Value" check out well, you can be reasonably certain that you are making a well-educated (if not entirely infallible) decision.

Authenticity

No matter how beautiful a work of art is, if you buy it and it turns out to be a fake, you have a major problem on your hands.

THE BEST OF EVERYTHING

Before you purchase a serious work, verifying its authenticity is obviously essential to both establishing its value and ensuring that its value will be retained.

Generally speaking, the more obvious the clues the less reliable they are. Labels on frames, certifications of authenticity, or any form of guarantee are only as good as the source. Walk into any one of thousands of art "galleries" across the country and you'll find plenty of lithographs and drawings purportedly signed by the likes of Salvador Dalí, Marc Chagall, Alexander Calder, Joan Miró, and Picasso. Unfortunately, customers mistakenly believe that these claims are sufficient to ensure that they are purchasing the genuine article. Yet there is no Good Housekeeping Seal of Approval to protect the collector. Nowhere is the time-honored warning *caveat emptor* more applicable than in the world of art.

Outright fakes and forgeries are certainly cause for concern, but they account for only a small fraction of all misrepresentations. Most are simply misattributions. A painting from a master's studio might be incorrectly attributed to the artist himself, or a work by a minor painter might innocently be attributed to a great one.

To a certain degree, the great artists are themselves responsible for this legacy of confusion. The French Rococo painter Boucher, the Flemish old master Rubens, and the French landscape painter Corot are only a few of the artists who signed works actually executed in their studios. Hence the line "Corot painted 1,000 pictures, 1,500 of which are in the United States."

So how do you protect yourself from fakes—intentional and otherwise? Since authenticity must always be a matter of general consensus and/or clear proof, it is wise to question assumptions by consulting the best reference works, comparing the piece with documented examples, and seeking out the advice and opinions (preferably in writing) of acknowledged experts in the field.

These experts have at their disposal a battery of scientific

HOW TO ASSESS VALUE: NINE DENOMINATORS

techniques to determine age and origin—carbon dating for antiquities (as in the T'ang horse affair), chemical tests to determine whether the varnish and the pigments used on a particular canvas match those used by the specific old master it is attributed to, and so on. Beyond all the laboratory tricks, the single most important asset an expert brings to this process is his trained eye.

A stunning example of just how important it is to establish authenticity beyond any doubt occurred in 1988, when an auction house sold a portrait of George Washington for $3,300 after it determined that the painting was definitely not the work of the famous American artist Gilbert Stuart. Three months later, after the same portrait was judged by other experts to be the real McCoy, it sold for $495,000. It was later learned that the painting had in fact once been owned by James Madison. There was even a label on the back saying so!

Fortunately, this sort of controversy about authenticity is rare. The individual who walks into the auction house with a question as to an item's authenticity can usually get a straight answer, and quickly. When a fourteen-year-old boy discovered an odd-looking mask made of wood and shaped like a seal's head in his grandmother's attic, the woman brought it to our expert on American Indian art. The expert was pleased to tell her and her grandson on the spot that they had uncovered an authentic Eskimo face mask. We sold it shortly thereafter for $28,000— enough to pay for a year at Harvard!

More often than not, however, people tend to vastly overvalue their family heirlooms. "My grandmother says this table came over on the *Mayflower*" and "George Washington sat in this chair" are familiar refrains, but it's awfully hard to get excited when the pieces are clearly Victorian.

Sometimes, though, things are not so clear-cut, as when the story and the item seem to match. Particularly in the area of Americana, hearsay is often all we have to go on in determining historical importance. We know that the top hat we sold for $10,000 belonged to Abraham Lincoln because generation after

This misidentified "copy" of a Gilbert Stuart,
bought in 1988 for just $3,300, turned
out to be the real thing.

generation told us this was so. But when there is even the slightest bit of doubt as to authenticity, we make that fact clear by saying, for instance, "This amber bead necklace is *reputed* to have been owned by Martha Washington." (Washington scholars must have been satisfied that it was, since Mount Vernon wound up acquiring the necklace from us in 1980.)

Finally, while authenticity is of utmost importance in determining the value of a specific object, remember that there is no shame in being duped. The Texas oilman Alger Meadows, who spent millions on Impressionist and Post-Impressionist paintings in the 1950s and 1960s, ultimately came to the realization that many of the marvelous "finds" he had come across were in fact skillfully executed forgeries. With the aid of a dealer, Meadows managed to rebuild his collection from the ground up.

Few connoisseurs, even those in search of shortcuts, have been so spectacularly deceived as Meadows. Nevertheless, I feel it is a truism that every great collector owns at least one fake. You have to be a little adventuresome in order to be an involved collector. Besides, if you're right *all* the time, you're probably being a little too cautious.

Condition

An acquaintance of mine was justifiably proud of the Picasso he had acquired in the late 1950s and asked me one day to drop by his East River apartment to take a look at it. When I was led into the living room where the drawing had hung for more than twenty years, I was saddened by what I found. The Picasso was indeed exquisite, or at least it must have been when the artist finished it. What hung there now was washed out and faded, ruined by years of exposure to direct sunlight. The drawing was undeniably one of Picasso's better efforts, but the owner's careless treatment of his masterpiece had reduced its value to a fraction of what it would have been.

THE BEST OF EVERYTHING

Anything less than perfect condition makes a difference. Certainly the degree of damage, repair, or restoration will vary and thus affect the value of the object in differing degrees. In essence, the closer an art work is found to be to its original perfect condition, the more it will retain its value.

When a major museum consigned Benvenuto di Giovanni's *The Assumption of the Virgin* to Sotheby's a few years ago, the 490-year-old painting would have sold easily for $500,000 had it not been clumsily "restored" twenty years earlier. Instead, it sold for $67,500.

Just how difficult it is to find something that even approximates its original condition is obvious in the case of the old masters. But keep in mind that an almost microscopic hairline crack in a piece of porcelain or a scratch in a tabletop can have the same disastrous effect. "Perfect condition" is often so hard to come by that it alone can sometimes be enough to make a work by a lesser artist more valuable.

The answer may seem to be restoration. Wrong! Repairs, restorations, and adaptations may enhance a work's outward appearance, but all these "improvements" often actually serve to undermine the item's integrity. An attempt to patch the thinning silver on the bottom of a Revere bowl, the gleaming new finish on the Queen Anne highboy, the "retouched" foreground of a canvas—all can detract seriously from the value of an individual object unless done with expert care.

Just how battered an object can be and still rate as a first-class antique was evident in the case of a wing chair I encountered a couple of years ago. A photograph was sent to Sotheby's for an appraisal; as is the case with many antiques, the chair in the picture looked as if it had been pulled from the back of a garbage truck. The upholstery was not just ripped, it was shredded. The owner felt the chair was worthless, but before he went ahead with plans to throw it away, he took a friend's advice to consult an expert.

What the owner did not know was that in the evaluation of

HOW TO ASSESS VALUE: NINE DENOMINATORS

American furniture, the frame is of primary importance—not the upholstery. The seedy-looking piece of furniture in the photograph turned out to be a Philadelphia Queen Anne shell carved walnut wing chair, and the original finish on the wood was in nearly perfect condition. Because no one had tampered with the chair, we had no difficulty at all selling it for $85,000. When it comes to furniture, a little benign neglect can work wonders.

Rarity

You may own a beautiful object of great quality and in perfect condition, but if it's only one of twenty thousand similar objects, it won't be worth very much. In a collecting world governed by the laws of supply and demand, the fewer good-quality items available in a collecting area, the greater the value.

Rarity can overtake all other factors in determining an object's market value. That sweetmeats dish that was purchased at a tag sale on Long Island for $4 and sold the next year for $66,000 was valuable for one reason: made in Philadelphia by Bonin and Morris, America's first and only eighteenth-century porcelain factory, the dish is one of three known to exist. Of the remaining two, one is in the Brooklyn Museum, the other at the Smithsonian.

A child's wooden sled could not be considered a work of art, unless it was the Rosebud sled used in the classic Orson Welles film *Citizen Kane*. Actually, there were two balsawood sleds used as props in the movie. One, as every film buff knows, was burned in the final scene of *Citizen Kane*. The director Steven Spielberg bought the other one at one of our collectibles sales for $55,000. It now hangs above his desk by way of providing the filmmaker with a little inspiration.

There are, of course, countless other examples of objects that command fortunes principally because of their extreme

The wood's the thing:
this battered Queen Anne shell
carved walnut wing chair
brought $85,000.

This rare eighteenth-century
Chippendale "hairy-paw foot" chair
commanded a record $275,000
in 1982, and would fetch
much more today.

rarity. In the automobile world, for example, there are only six 16-cylinder Bugatti Royales in existence, making each worth more than $8 million. Among American bronzes, there are only three known casts of Frederic Remington's *The Norther,* the last sold in 1987 to an American museum for $715,000. The greatest illuminated manuscript in private hands, *The Gospels of Henry the Lion,* is one of the most lavish examples of Romanesque art anywhere—and the rarest, making it worth $12 million to West Germany when it was sold at auction in 1985. And among jewels, Kashmir sapphires are worth a fortune not only because of their deep blue velvety color, but because the Himalayan mines that produced them were closed to all foreigners in 1883.

Rarity is almost always a plus, though strangely enough, it is possible for an object to be too rare. If you own the only existing example of something, that's all well and good providing there is someone else who would be interested in owning it too. You must, in other words, have a strong secondary market. Collecting signed prints in limited editions of 30 to 300 has become very popular in recent years precisely because the supply is controlled but enough prints are kept circulating out there in the marketplace to stimulate demand.

Historic Importance and Provenance

There are times when an object's appeal rests entirely or at least in part on its historic value. The top hat Abraham Lincoln wore to Ford's Theater the night of his assassination, for example, was worth the $10,000 paid for it at auction in 1979 solely because of its historic association. The same can be said for George Washington's Valley Forge campstool (sold to the Smithsonian in 1976 for $12,500); the $1.15 million handwritten manuscript of Einstein's theory of relativity; the only signed and dated version of the Gettysburg Address (sold at Sotheby's in 1950 for $54,000);

and Napoleon Bonaparte's four-page outline of his plans to invade England, which sold in December of 1988 for the surprisingly modest price of $21,186.

My personal favorite is the bill Paul Revere submitted for one of his famous rides. The handwritten document (which we sold to Malcolm Forbes from the Sang collection in 1978 for $70,000) includes the feeding of Revere's horse, Revere's hotel bill, the horse's time, and Revere's time. The bill was made payable to John Hancock, who had advanced Revere the funds. Apparently Hancock had been in charge of petty cash.

Historic importance may also be loosely interpreted to apply to certain collectibles. The upright piano from *Casablanca,* which Sotheby's sold in 1988 for $140,000, occupies a legitimate place in the history of motion pictures, as do the boat from *The African Queen* and the boxing gloves worn by Sylvester Stallone in *Rocky.*

Sometimes historic importance accounts for only a portion of an item's worth. While the bill for Paul Revere's ride is purely of historic interest, the silver he crafted is valuable on aesthetic as well as historic grounds. Other silversmiths of the period may have been just as talented, but because of Revere's reputation as a patriot his bowls, mugs, coffeepots, and candlesticks command prices far higher than those by his contemporaries. In 1976, for example, Sotheby's sold a Revere silver tankard, standing 8½ inches tall, for $45,000. (A cautionary note: The initials "P.R." on a piece of old silver should be viewed with considerable suspicion. Artful forgers have had two centuries now to perfect their craft, and if they are going to copy any silversmith, it's Paul.)

Similarly, as fine a painter as Gilbert Stuart was, his best-known portrait is of George Washington, not of some unknown colonist. The same rule applies to Emmanuel Leutze's *George Washington Crossing the Delaware.* The historical component here is so great that in 1980 I even sold a copy of the famous painting, albeit by Eastman Johnson, for $370,000.

Historic importance, however, has nothing to do with who

has owned the work, or its "provenance." But a work's provenance can likewise greatly increase its worth. For example, the value of an eighteenth-century French console soars when Sotheby's discovers an inventory mark that firmly establishes it as once being the property of Marie Antoinette. A Milanese suit of armor made by Negroli in 1545 for Henry II, who was five-foot-two, brings $3 million at auction. A pair of Elton John's eyeglasses sells for $16,830; a sweat-stained jumpsuit worn by Elvis Presley goes for $44,800; and buyers hungrily bid for a Cartier sapphire and diamond clip owned by the Duchess of Windsor before someone wins it for nearly $1.3 million. Then there are the two Andy Warhol cookie jars that someone thought were worth $23,100.

None of these items has true historic value, and often the artistic value is marginal, if it can be ascertained at all. What creates the intense competition is the fact that the objects were owned, handled, and appreciated by somebody famous.

Provenance. The history of ownership. Who possessed an object and when. Where it has been. These factors can have a significant effect on value. They also help in establishing a work's authenticity while adding luster—a dash of glamour by association with a famous name.

This is not a new phenomenon. Almost two centuries ago, Christie's found a healthy market for the studio contents of such artists as Sir Joshua Reynolds and Thomas Gainsborough. Jerome Kern's collection of autographs and rare books set a long-standing record of $1.7 million in 1929. The trend gathered momentum in the 1960s as larger and larger numbers of people came to value the possessions of the famous—from the cosmetics queen Helena Rubinstein's Russian icons, Victorian settees, and African masks to Cole Porter's bejeweled cigarette cases.

Whether people were motivated by nostalgia or vicarious interest in the life-styles of the rich and famous, celebrity auctions took off in the 1980s as thousands flocked to see and bid for everything from Shirley Temple's teddy bear to John Lennon's psychedelic Rolls-Royce.

HOW TO ASSESS VALUE: NINE DENOMINATORS

But there are times when provenance can assure the artistic integrity of a work and thus legitimately boost its value. That is the case when a painting has been in a museum collection, say, or has been owned by a prestigious collector, such as Paul Mellon or Norton Simon. Provenance of this kind can go a long way toward dispelling lingering doubts as to authenticity or quality. If you are breeding show dogs, you look for a pedigree. When you collect, you look for provenance. The same fundamental theory applies.

This principle was certainly true in the case of Florence Gould. Mrs. Gould was a leading hostess in France, a patron of the arts, and an arbiter of taste in the art world; her special passion was the Impressionists. When we auctioned her collection in April of 1985, the mere fact that these paintings hung on her walls doubled the interest in the sale.

That night, records toppled like dominoes. I hammered down Toulouse-Lautrec's portrait *The Clowness Cha-u-Kao,* one of his favorite dancers from the Moulin Rouge, for $5,280,000, a record for the artist. Later, *Landscape with Rising Sun,* painted from van Gogh's window at the asylum in Saint-Remy, went for $9.9 million—an auction record for the artist and for a Post-Impressionist up to that time. After two hours of frenzied bidding, the total for the evening was $36.2 million. By association with Mrs. Gould, the collection commanded a ready market for well-known paintings and gave lesser works a decided boost. Provenance was clearly an important component in the success of that remarkable auction.

By extension, the new collector feels more comfortable just knowing that the item he is being asked to bid $5,000 for was once owned by a celebrity. Of course, provenance often has little to do with quality. Buying a rhinestone-covered glove once worn by Michael Jackson is one thing. Assuming that a painting from a rock star's private collection is really worth the fortune being asked for it is quite another.

Provenance can have its downside as well. When he acquired the dark blue 45.52-carat Hope Diamond as part of the estate of

Evalyn Walsh McLean in 1949, Harry Winston was practically the only person who wasn't convinced that he would fall victim to the diamond's famous "curse."

Soon after he purchased the gem, Winston and his wife, Edna, were vacationing in Lisbon when Mrs. Winston decided to take an early plane home to New York. When the man sitting next to her on the plane found out just before takeoff that she was Mrs. Harry Winston, he jumped out of his seat and talked the stewardess into letting him off the plane.

Later that night, Winston himself was on a second flight over the Atlantic when the man in the next seat turned to him and said, "Whew, I almost got stuck on a plane with the wife of that guy who owns the Hope Diamond." It was the same man! Winston didn't have the heart to tell the worried stranger who he was.

Winston later donated the Hope Diamond to the Smithsonian, where it is on display. (It cost him $2.44 to send the one-of-a-kind jewel by registered mail.) Because it has been off the market for nearly forty years, there is no way to tell what the Hope Diamond might bring if it were offered at auction today. But there is little question that the famous curse adds considerably to its luster.

In weighing the importance of provenance, a good rule of thumb is to first judge the object on its own merits. Strip it of its past. Once you have established in your mind what a fair price might be, then factor in the name value of the previous owner(s). This can be a daunting task even for the experts. There is no way we could have anticipated that Andy Warhol's kitsch would bring twice what we predicted or that the Duchess of Windsor's gems would sell for seven times our presale estimate. Better that, though, than the other way around. . . .

There are times when the lore behind the acquisition of a piece, without affecting value in any way, can bring an added dimension to the business of collecting. As he walked to work each day, a friend of mine could not help but notice the haunting portrait of a sixteenth-century English cleric that seemed to beckon to him from the window of an antiques shop. One day, he went into the store, and after one of the shop's two owners agreed to reduce the price, he went ahead and bought it. A little restoration had to be done, so my friend agreed to come back a couple of days later to pick up the painting.

When he returned for the portrait, he noticed that the hand of one of the store owners was bandaged. It turned out that the two men, who had been in business together for thirty years, had fought bitterly over whether to sell the painting at a reduced price; one of the partners had actually attacked the other with a pair of scissors. Within a few weeks, the business closed and a jewelry store opened in its place.

My friend then did some research about the man in the painting and discovered that he not only had been Henry VIII's chaplain and the bishop of London but had conspired with Lady Jane Grey to seize the throne—a crime for which he was burned at the stake by "Bloody Mary" Tudor. Such a tale probably has little to do with the value of the work historically or in terms of provenance, but there is much fun to be had in the telling.

Size

Value cannot be computed by square inches, but it can be said that collectors are not likely to get terribly excited about a Renoir two inches by two inches. By the same token, apartment dwellers with eight-foot ceilings might understandably look askance at a looming ten-foot by four-foot eighteenth-century English portrait.

The same applies to furniture. While most of us have scaled down our living quarters in recent years, the market has similarly shrunk for those Brobdingnagian credenzas and massive desks that filled the baronial mansions of the rich. Even the oversized

*The Duke and Duchess of Windsor
on their wedding day. She wears a bracelet
enscribed "For Our Contract 18-V-37,"
which later became a centerpiece of the
landmark auction of her jewelry.*

Victorian chairs and heavy tables that used to fit so perfectly into Grandma's big, drafty old house would seem obscenely prepossessing—if not outright silly—in most of today's suburban family dwellings. In general, it is probably a good idea to stay away from extremes in size.

There are, of course, exceptions. All other things being equal, I have never heard anyone complain that a diamond was too big. At the other end of the spectrum, there are certain collecting areas—netsuke, snuff boxes, miniature portraiture, even some Fabergé items—where the detail of the craftsmanship is so fine that the prevailing rule is the tinier the better.

In recent years, the obsession with the not-so-grand has led to a virtual explosion in the area of dollhouse furniture. The amounts devoted collectors are willing to spend on these precious miniature cabinets and secretaries (some of which were used as samples by the leading furniture makers of the eighteenth century) are anything but small. In 1980, a spice cabinet fashioned in the form of a tiny highboy was purchased for $65,000—probably more than the full-size version would have cost.

Medium

The materials used to create a work of art or an antique will have an effect, often a substantial one, on value. Oil paintings, for instance, are more valuable than watercolors. This is because oils are a more demanding medium for the artist to work in, and they last longer. After watercolors come drawings; after drawings, prints. Pastel drawings are the least durable of the various media, but they can still command high prices, especially when an artist is identified with that particular medium. In 1988, I sold a Degas pastel for $7.5 million.

As with paintings, each collecting area has its own pecking

order vis-à-vis medium. Bronze sculptures, of course, tend to be more valuable than wooden ones. In the field of jewelry, the medium *is* the message. Sapphires are less prized than rubies, rubies less than emeralds, and emeralds usually take a back seat to diamonds. If there are no differences in size, quality, design, provenance, and so on, a jewel in a platinum setting will be more highly prized than one set in gold.

When evaluating a piece of furniture, we look not at the upholstery but at the wood. Since mahogany is imported, American mahogany furniture is nearly always more desirable (and hence more expensive) than, say, home-grown walnut, cherry, maple, or pine. In short, if you have two chairs identical in craftsmanship and in every other way, value pretty much becomes a question of the materials used. Yet two items are rarely identical in every other way, and other considerations are likely to have a much greater impact on what that chair is worth. Antiques, after all, are more than a matter of lumber.

In assessing value, be certain to factor in the medium. But if most of the value of an item is due to the basic materials, then you are purchasing a commodity, not a work of art.

Subject Matter

The subject depicted in a work of art can have a great deal to do with what it will bring on the open market. People have very specific tastes—the Japanese buyers, for instance, have a decided preference for figurative nudes—but there are some general rules that seem to apply to art buyers' taste as a whole. A Rembrandt painting of a dead ox will in all likelihood not be as valuable as a Rembrandt portrait of a lovely young girl. Most people would still rather look at (and own) a picture of an attractive woman than a portrait of a grim, scowling male. If you have two Renoirs painted in the same month, and one is a voluptuous nude sitting on a rock by a stream and the other is a vase of flowers, the nude will win. Hands down.

In fact, a beautiful young woman is the most desirable of all subjects. At a recent Impressionist sale, one Mary Cassatt sold for about $450,000—far less than the minimum estimate—while another brought more than $2 million. The first was a portrait of a rather bland-looking, middle-aged woman, and frankly, the owner was eager to sell it. The other was a picture of a radiant little blond girl holding a dog in her lap. The buyer told me later that the child reminded him of his daughter. It was a painting, in short, he would not mind looking at forever. Subject matter was the deciding factor here.

Even if the subject is not particularly beautiful, most people find a portrait of a female more appealing than one of a male. Youth, in terms of subject matter at least, is better than age. Among males, young men in military uniform tend to fetch higher prices. In the animal kingdom, live is preferable to dead. Among still lifes, most people favor flowers to fruit. A spring landscape is invariably preferred to a snowy scene.

As for the emotions depicted in a painting, love, joy, and passion can be listed in the asset column. Angst, pain, violence, and ugliness of any kind go down as liabilities. Most of us would rather be uplifted by the art we own than depressed by it.

After this explanation of the pecking order, suffice it to say that there are countless exceptions to the rule—particularly since many great artists are strongly identified with specific subject matter. Gauguin's Tahitian women fit into the pecking order rather nicely, as do Degas's dancers. But how do you explain that Monet's water lilies are as prized as his seascapes, that Cézanne is synonymous with still lifes of fruit, and that the, costliest painting in history was not of a gorgeous sylph but van Gogh's *Irises?* What of Rubens's bloody hunting scenes, El Greco's contorted limbs, Munch's screaming faces, Botero's bloated Babbitts, Dalí's surreal dreams, or, for that matter, Warhol's soup cans?

If the artist isn't clearly identified with a specific subject, then value will be determined to some degree by our gut reaction to the piece. If you're going to be living with something for a long time, you want to be sure of one thing above all else—that it pleases you.

Fashion

Some things never seem to go out of fashion. Fine old master paintings, for instance. Queen Anne and Chippendale furniture, classic French furniture, American silver, gems. Nonetheless, just as a glamour stock can go out of fashion, art can too. It is a risk you the collector must be aware of.

The continuing evolution of taste and aesthetic theory will have an effect on the price of paintings, drawings, sculpture, antiques, and collectibles as an area's importance is established or reassessed over the years. A few artists from every period may reach a level that gives them a certain immunity to shifts in taste, but most are subject to the vagaries of fashion. As an earlier style comes back into vogue among collectors, prices begin to rise accordingly.

Conversely, when a style falls from favor, prices plummet. An entire category that may be regarded as aesthetically superior today can be ruthlessly demoted tomorrow by a change in the prevailing aesthetic theory. Nothing need be "wrong" with the work, and nothing is different about it. Only the perception of its value by the collecting community has changed. It has simply been reassessed.

The best example of this is the Impressionists, who were laughed at when their paintings were exhibited for the first time in the United States in 1893. Had anyone had the foresight to buy them, the paintings shown during that exhibition alone could have been the foundation for the greatest museum in the world today. Similarly, critics derisively called Matisse, Georges Braque,

Raoul Dufy, Maurice de Vlaminck, Georges Rouault, and Kees van Dongen *fauves* (from the French, meaning "wild beast") because they were supposedly nothing less than madmen for painting the way they did. Their distorted forms, executed in exuberant colors, were thought at the time to be almost infantile. Today, of course, *fauve* is a magic word, with those names commanding some of the highest prices in the auction world.

The Barbizon school of mid-nineteenth-century French landscape painting took a similar roller-coaster ride. At the turn of the twentieth century this was the most popular style to buy, but over time it was rejected. People got tired of the cows and sheep and all the rest. In recent years, it has undergone a great renaissance, since the ingredients for success are there: high-quality paintings in good supply, at reasonable prices.

Changing times also had a profound impact on seventeenth- and eighteenth-century portraiture, which was very popular in the 1920s and 1930s. Back then, people in search of status enthusiastically collected portraits of other people's ancestors, by such top-of-the-line artists as Gilbert Stuart and John Singleton Copley, to pass off as their own. Today, we don't feel the need to hang ancestors on our walls, so these portraits have to stand on their own as works of art. With the exception of works by such artists as Thomas Gainsborough, Joshua Reynolds, and a handful of other great British portraitists, those magnificent, larger-than-life studies that hung in English country homes took a downturn in the 1970s and 1980s. English portraiture from the eighteenth and the early nineteenth centuries is now worth substantially less than it was in the 1920s.

Will portraiture come back into fashion, just as the Barbizon school eventually did? With its extravagant color and light and the marvelous texture, it really is no wonder that English portraiture is already making a major comeback. As for its more somber American counterpart, well, it depends. The public today is much more intellectually involved with the subject than previous generations, searching for something that will enhance the quality of their own lives. This may include our ancestors, but the rather humorless faces that stare back at us often offer little sustenance for the soul. Still, if the sitter is attractive and the portrait is well painted, it will always find a ready market.

If you are feeling a patriotic twinge, take heart. Nearly everything else American is very much in fashion these days. The American Impressionists, long eclipsed by their European cousins, are now much in demand. Even the WPA Depression painters, muralists, and sculptors, whose work was viewed as far too populist to be considered "art," are now avidly sought by serious collectors. It took a while, but the art world finally realized that this was an entire new school, born of a unique place and time.

Trends are sometimes started by influential individuals. Baroque furnishings became the rage in the 1920s after William Randolph Hearst went on a buying binge to fill up San Simeon, and John Gaines almost single-handedly revived interest in old master drawings.

When Prince Charles proposed to Lady Diana Spencer, the engagement ring he gave her—a large oval sapphire surrounded by diamonds—became one of the most photographed pieces of jewelry in history. Overnight, sapphire prices soared. Similarly, the Duchess of Windsor sale spawned an interest in animal pins.

Wallis Warfield is not alone among posthumous trendsetters. Puiforcat French silver was not exactly a household word until Andy Warhol's sizable collection of Puiforcat—in fact, the largest collection of Puiforcat—came on the market as part of the Warhol sale in 1988. Prices for the elegant French silver skyrocketed, and a new market was created.

In the world of furniture, a handful of interior designers exert a palpable influence on what people will collect. When Mario Buatta and Mark Hampton decreed that the English country gentleman look was in and filled their rooms with chintz, tassels, leather, and overstuffed chairs, this trend coincided with a surge in auction prices for English antiques.

Perhaps no one is more responsible for popularizing the

classic, solid English and Early American look than the fashion designer Ralph Lauren. What goes better with a double-breasted wool blazer than a George I walnut wing chair or a Regency mahogany writing table?

Just as it can boost the market value of a specific artist's work, a blockbuster museum show can also start a broader, more comprehensive trend—witness the effect of Tut on Egyptiana, of Brooke Astor's wing at the Metropolitan on Chinese art, and so on.

More often than not, however, the finger of fashion is fickle indeed. Oriental art was highly fashionable in the early part of the nineteenth century, died in the mid-1800s, rebounded at the turn of the twentieth century, vanished again, returned again. Tiffany glass, Art Nouveau, and Art Deco have all been carried on the tides of fashion. Why are jukeboxes in one year and out the next? Is there any logical reason behind the shift from emerald-cut diamonds in the 1940s and 1950s to marquise- and brilliant-cut in the 1980s? Or from white diamonds to "fancy" diamonds in various hues of yellow, pink, and blue? One might just as well ask why they no longer make cars with tail fins.

Predicting what is likely to stay in style is the hard part. In making judgments, dispense with the faddish and trendy. For example, the Nehru jacket became very popular in the late 1960s, but taste ruled this article of clothing out as fashion, relegating it to the status of a passing fad. Conversely, blue jeans started out as purely functional attire but were adopted by American youth as a kind of uniform. Eventually, they became a timeless classic of American fashion.

Try to imagine how an object will stand the test of time. Will people appreciate it in the year 2000? How about a hundred years from now? As with talent, quality will out.

Aesthetic Quality

Monet painted scores of *Nymphéas* over a period of years, but some are considered outstanding while others are relatively mediocre. Two Cézanne paintings made in the same month may be of radically different quality. Even Picasso had his bad days.

Aesthetic quality is at once the most important and the least easily defined of all the criteria for selecting a work of art. But demand it you must. In fact, you owe it to yourself to apply the highest standards in determining aesthetic quality; it's your money you're spending, so be ruthless. As Somerset Maugham once said, "If you refuse to accept anything but the best, you very often get it."

First, though, you must be able to recognize the best when you see it. You cannot define quality by simply adding up other criteria of value. After you have carefully taken into account such factors as authenticity, condition, rarity, historic importance, provenance, size, medium, subject matter, and fashion, you are left to make a relatively subjective judgment as to quality.

I say "relatively subjective" because to a certain extent there is an almost objective way to judge the quality of a work. The expert and the knowledgeable collector, having immersed themselves in a particular subject and possessing a knowledge of how a work stands up against comparable objects, bring to the process of judging what is popularly known as an "eye" for quality.

Can such an eye be acquired? I am convinced, genetics aside, that the development of taste is a question of environment. You are not born with an ability to cull the wheat from the chaff. The eye can be educated to differentiate between good and bad. Becoming a successful collector is a never-ending process aimed at refining your expertise in a chosen area. In collecting, knowledge is truly power. With it, you can take your first bold steps on the exciting journey toward becoming a connoisseur.

CHAPTER — FIVE

Getting Started:
The Road to
Connoisseurship

Renoir once supposedly asked Cézanne, "How can you wear that cravat? Can't you see it's in bad taste?"

"If it were in bad taste," Cézanne replied, "I wouldn't be wearing it."

Without question, a degree of confidence is necessary to become a connoisseur, but so are knowledge, experience, and discrimination. These the true connoisseur has in abundance.

Traditionally, the connoisseur has always also had an ample supply of something else: wealth. Names like Rockefeller, Dodge, Mellon, Widener, Hearst, and Vanderbilt dominated the ranks of collectors for most of this century. Edith Rockefeller McCormick, daughter of John D. Rockefeller and daugher-in-law of the

"Reaper King" Cyrus McCormick, lived so formally that, even when she dined alone, her menus were printed in French with gold ink on special paper. As recently as the mid-1970s, whenever we had an important painting for sale, I would write down on a piece of paper the names of the likely bidders—all ten of them! I was rarely wrong in those days.

All that has changed dramatically. Today virtually anyone with a few thousand dollars to spend, a passion to collect, and a desire to learn can become a connoisseur. Whether we are investing $5,000 or $50 million, each of us has a unique style. This ensures that, like sets of fingerprints, no two collections are exactly alike.

Connoisseurs come in as many varieties as the artists they collect. They might be traditional or avant-garde, maverick or erudite, ironic or realist, intellectual or mystical. The list of adjectives to describe them is endless, but when it comes to the modus operandi, all fall into two broad categories.

One type of connoisseur has an almost reverential concern for history, and builds a collection around a particular concept, period, or movement. Obeying all the rules, he or she collects only French Impressionists or only American Shaker furniture. But the modus operandi, or M.O., of the other type, the instinctive collector, is quite different. He or she is, in contrast, something of a loose cannon. The instinctive collector chooses artists in a manner that might seem impulsive, even arbitrary.

What both breeds of collector share is great passion and a willingness to immerse themselves in it. The instinctive collector may be more apt to follow his heart, but he is usually no less knowledgeable than his more predictable counterpart. He is schooled in the nine denominators of value discussed here. But —and this is just as important to him—he knows what he likes.

One of the perks of my job is that I get to store many of the items slated for auction in my office, which thus becomes a kind of mini-gallery with revolving exhibits of the world's great art trea-

THE ROAD TO CONNOISSEURSHIP

sures. On the wall behind my desk often hangs the pick of the next major auction. It might be a Picasso one week, a Whistler the next. A permanent feature is my bronze bust of Lincoln, wearing a golf cap at a rakish angle.

When the $2.75 million General Cadwalader hairy-paw foot wing armchair was being offered, as a lover of American furniture I naturally was happy to keep it in my office. During the weeks before the auction, a steady stream of American furniture collectors, connoisseurs, and curators came to Sotheby's to see "the chair," and they were escorted to my office.

After an exchange of pleasantries, I was amused to see these groups of otherwise reserved, distinguished, and well-dressed visitors get down on all fours and start crawling around on the floor to get a better look. Invariably, at least one member of each group would turn over on his back and scoot up beneath the chair to better scrutinize its underside. While the workshop where the chair was made was known to us, one expert emerged from his floor-level examination with the news that he had actually pinpointed the name of the chair's carver.

At these times my office and I ceased to exist. The communion between these collectors and this chair was so intense that for those precious moments everything else in the world was shut out. For these people, the General Cadwalader hairy-paw foot wing armchair was the Holy Grail.

To me, this is the pure definition of connoisseurship and, by extension, of collecting: to be so in awe of the significance, rarity, and aesthetics of a particular work that the work itself inspires a kind of reverence. This represents years of the observer's scholarship intersecting with years of the creator's artistic refinement, culminating in an almost magical moment of appreciation.

Connoisseurship is not so much a destination as it is a journey, and the better equipped you become at each stage the more you are able to enjoy the trip. While there are no shortcuts, you should know how to get off to the proper start and be aware of some of the more productive routes to take.

The Acquisitive Mind

Is everybody cut out to become a serious collector? Absolutely not. We all know people who are perfectly happy going about their lives without really giving any active thought to the beauty that surrounds them. Even people with a finely honed aesthetic sense may not have any proprietary inclinations toward art. They may not feel the need to possess beautiful objects so long as they can see them in museums or reproduced in the pages of coffee table books.

For the true collector, however, there can be no adequate substitute for *owning* something exquisite, whether it is an Andrew Wyeth print, a grandfather clock, a piece of French porcelain, or a paperweight. These are the people who were born with an acquisitive nature. Perhaps they were lucky enough to get started early and to build up their collection steadily. Or, as is more often the case, they waited until they had the time and the means to join in the pursuit of all things bright and beautiful.

It is fascinating how many great collectors can trace their passion for collecting back to childhood, when they amassed vast treasures in bottle tops, toy soldiers, baseball cards, and, in my case, little hotel soaps. Joe Hirshhorn started collecting calendars, graduated to reproductions of paintings used for the calendars, and then to the original works themselves before becoming one of history's greatest modern art collectors.

J. K. Lilly, the pharmaceuticals giant, began by collecting toy soldiers, then gold coins, then stamps and jewels. All were stored in vaults and hauled out on occasion strictly for his personal enjoyment. Much later in life, he accumulated old master paintings that now form an important part of the collection of the Indianapolis Institute of Fine Art.

John Ryan Gaines, son of the founder of the Gaines dog food company, collected stamps as a boy, then put this hobby aside for several decades to pursue his love of horses. A top Kentucky breeder by the 1970s, he wandered into Parke-Bernet one day and found himself drawn to an auction lot of Japanese prints. Gaines later told me that back then he "didn't know a Hokusai from an Utamaro." (Utamaro is known for his portraits of women, Hokusai for dreamy landscapes.) What he did know was that he was smitten, and that day he bought the lot. "There's nothing," he said, "like jumping off the end of the diving board for learning to swim." The purchase of the lot of Japanese prints marked the beginning of Gaines's education as a connoisseur. That path took a different turn, however, when, in 1972, he paid $38,000 for a sheet of drawings done by Agostino Carracci in 1600.

After fourteen years, Gaines figured it was time to sell his collection, so he consigned forty-six master drawings to Sotheby's. The sale cleared $21.3 million, setting record prices for twenty-seven old master and modern drawings by such artists as Rembrandt, Turner, Watteau, Picasso, Delacroix, Leonardo, and Millet. The Carracci was also sold, for $363,000—ten times Gaines's purchase price.

What struck me about Gaines's collection at that time was its consistently high quality and its breadth. It is clear that Gaines, in putting together his collection, had not compromised in his search for the finest examples of each period and style from the fifteenth century to the twentieth. Leonardo da Vinci's dual interest in the scientific as well as the artistic was evident in the sheet of studies Gaines had selected. On one side were three sketches of a child holding a lamb, in black chalk, pen, and brown ink; on the other side were studies of machinery and several lines of explanatory text in Leonardo's trademark mirror writing.

To represent the best of Rembrandt's skill as a draftsman, Gaines had picked two of the artist's landscapes in pen and gray-brown wash. Other artists were represented by the subjects with which they are synonymous—Degas's dancers, Millet's sower, Gainsborough's aristocratic ladies. But what establishes Gaines's eye for quality is his ability to see beyond the obvious and expected. Picasso's drawing, *Man with a Pipe,* for example, marks a break from the constraints of analytical Cubism.

Over the years, John Gaines has assembled a number of different superb collections—mostly paintings, drawings, and prints. His approach to these collections reflects the consummate horse breeder's mentality: once a collection is sired and reared, it is sold at auction.

Like every great connoisseur I've known, Gaines speaks of collecting as his passion. The true collector will stop at next to nothing for the perfect example of whatever it is that stirs that passion, be it fishing tackle, tapestries, or salt and pepper shakers. It is hard to imagine anyone going to greater lengths than Mrs. John Rovensky, who in 1916 actually exchanged her Fifth Avenue mansion for two strands of superb matched natural pearls. Unfortunately for Mrs. Rovensky, real estate turned out to be a far wiser investment than Oriental pearls. The trade was made with Cartier, and that building is to this day the New York headquarters of the prestigious firm. The introduction of cultured pearls sent her pearl necklaces plummeting in value; when her estate was sold in 1959, they fetched $155,000, a pittance compared to the prime commercial property that she bartered away—her former home—now worth tens of millions.

The film producer Daniel Melnick has a magnificent obsession of his own. When a fellow collector of Northwest Coast art raved about the carvings of the Native American artist George David, Melnick boarded a flight in Los Angeles, changed planes several times, and finally took a puddle jumper to a remote island in the middle of Washington state's Neah Bay. There he convinced David to create two thirty-foot-high totem poles—a project that took two years and ended when Melnick had the totem poles loaded onto a flatbed truck, driven to L.A., and hoisted into position by crane above his house.

Consummately instinctive as a collector ("idiosyncratic, serendipitous, wildly eclectic" are his own words to describe his tastes), Melnick has interests that extend to African tribal shields, Thai heads, and the works of such modern masters as Jean Dubuffet, Ben Shahn, Fernand Léger, David Hockney, Roy Lichtenstein, Ellsworth Kelly, and Louise Nevelson.

Melnick has traced his interest in art back to his childhood in Manhattan, where he haunted the Museum of Modern Art and the Met. He bought a Giacometti with his first paycheck and by his mid-twenties was allotting a significant portion of his annual income to the acquisition of paintings and sculpture—laying the groundwork for a collection that would be worth hundreds of times his initial investment. "I've never bought anything strictly because I thought it was rare or historically interesting," he has explained. Ultimately, it all came down to aesthetics. "I never bought anything," Melnick has said with a shrug, "that I didn't think was beautiful."

The Consummate Connoisseur

No one has been more dedicated in his quest for quality than CBS founder William S. Paley. More than any other figure in the history of the medium, Paley brought quality to network programming—from legendary talents like Jack Benny, Bing Crosby, and Lucille Ball to a news department that has always been highly respected, with newscasters like Edward R. Murrow and Walter Cronkite leading the way.

It is in the realm of all things visual that Paley, an unrepentant perfectionist, truly excels. The Manhattan headquarters of CBS, affectionately known as Black Rock, is a case in point. It took more than a year before Paley approved the type of graphite-black granite to be used for the building's exterior (at one point the chairman of the board's corner office in CBS's old headquarters was crammed with seventy-five sample slabs of granite). Even then, he insisted that a full-scale mock-up of one corner be constructed before giving the final go-ahead; two mock-ups were built and torn down before he was satisfied with the third try.

Paley is quick to point out that Black Rock is, at thirty-five stories, "not big by New York standards, and it's not ostentatious. If quality is the right combination of materials, style, craftsmanship, and performance, then that's what it's got. We were striving for perfection, and I think we almost achieved it."

Paley was equally demanding about what went inside. No less an expert than his late wife, Babe Paley—a member of the Fashion Hall of Fame, whose own name was synonymous with style —once told her husband that he knew "how to arrange a room better than anyone." For Paley, that means "no interior decorators—too rigid. I like to mix things."

In searching for a word to describe Paley's office decor, "eclectic" would be a decided understatement. Instead of a desk, Paley works either at a stand-up lectern or a round eighteenth-century *chemin de fer* table that he discovered at an antiques shop in Paris. Nearby is what can best be described as a forerunner of the Barcalounger—an ornately carved nineteenth-century reclining chair with wooden arms that extend to become footrests.

As might be expected, there are also the mementos of six decades in broadcasting: antique microphones from CBS's original handful of member stations, the stopwatch seen at the beginning of "60 Minutes," a smattering of Emmys (including the coveted Governor's Award of the Television Academy of Arts and Sciences for lifetime achievement), a set of dog tags encased in plastic presented in gratitude from the cast and crew of "M*A*S*H" to commemorate the series' final episode—the single most watched program in television history. Gazing stoically over all this is a century-old cigar store Indian—a gift from Babe. "I don't want you to forget," she had told Paley, whose cigar-manufacturer father gave him the $400,000 to start CBS in 1928, "what business you started out in."

The three Picassos and the Franz Kline abstract painting that hang in Paley's CBS office offer only a small taste of one of the finest private collections anywhere. All of which should be expected: for many years Paley was chairman of the Museum of Modern Art, and afterward he continued to sit on MOMA's board of directors.

At Paley's Manhattan apartment and his Southampton estate the walls vibrate with the works of virtually every major Impressionist and Post-Impressionist except van Gogh. After the sale of *Irises,* he observed, "There just aren't any really good ones available."

As in all things, Paley's tastes in artists have evolved over time. "Gradually, Matisse has become my favorite painter. At one time it was Cézanne, without question. Picasso I put in a separate category. He's incapable of making a mistake." What pleases Paley most about collecting is that it serves as an outlet for personal expression. "People who have seen my collection," he explains, "have told me it has a character all its own, that you can tell one man put it all together. I like that."

For Paley, quality cannot be defined as simply a matter of personal taste: "Quality is something you have to see and to feel. When you do, it doesn't mean everybody sees it and feels it too. Quality is something you can't describe, but you recognize it when it comes along."

Being able to discern the mediocre from the exceptional, Paley says, is "an ability I treasure very much, and it permeates every part of my life. I feel very sorry for people who don't recognize quality and respond to it." For those who do want to sharpen their instincts, Paley offers some pointers: "If you see something that pleases you, get to know more about it. Then, when you say you know what you like and what you don't like, at least you'll be able to say it with conviction."

Paley cautions beginning collectors not to throw money at a work of art or antique purely for status reasons. Or to assume that you must have a fortune at your disposal to become a connoisseur. Even Australia's Alan Bond, who paid more money for a work of art than anyone else had when he bought van Gogh's *Irises* for $53.9 million, is quick to point out that money is not the key to becoming a true collector. "You can't just go out and buy a collection," says Bond, who started collecting French Impressionists and Australian art twenty years ago, before he turned thirty. "It takes years and years to put a collection together. You can't go out and buy it like a new suit of clothes."

If you have only a few thousand discretionary dollars to invest, then you have at your disposal all that it takes to buy the best of something. You can always afford to buy the best of whatever it is you can afford. "To me the terms 'highbrow' and 'quality' are not the same thing," explains Paley. "A lot that passes for quality is simply pretentious. As far as I'm concerned, the finest caviar in the world cannot compare with the American hot dog."

Despite their widely varied tastes and methods of operation, connoisseurs share a commitment to their chosen area of interest. There is only one way to determine beyond a doubt that you have the will to make such a commitment, and that is simply to take the plunge, to put your money where your heart is—always keeping in mind that you are only a student and bound to make a mistake or two along the way. But how else will you learn?

Pick Your Passion Carefully

A collecting area, be it coins or antiques or vintage cars, *must* pique your curiosity. It has to be something that you react to in a visceral way, something that you can develop an emotional attachment to. Not so much a single object, mind you. We all have a favorite pair of slippers or a favorite coffee mug, but that doesn't mean we should start collecting footwear and cups. It is a certain *type* of object that fascinates you, that you have an indefinable identification with, and that you—sometimes quite inexplicably—wish to possess.

THE ROAD TO CONNOISSEURSHIP

"For me," Daniel Melnick once explained, "collecting is about seeing something that deeply moves, challenges, or, on occasion, upsets me—and knowing that if I don't buy it, I'm not going to be able to spend enough time with the object to figure out what the experience means to me. Knowing that I haven't solved or internalized it yet, I want to be able to go on looking at the work. Why am I upset? Why do I want to laugh? When the mystery has been solved, it becomes less significant for me."

Since the area you choose is in effect an expression of you, nothing is too outrageous, too trivial to collect—providing there is someone out there to share your interest. Those people who collect barbed wire must top anyone's list in the strange-but-true category, but there are plenty of runners-up. Sotheby's publishes an annual catalogue for scientific instruments and another for those who collect old golf clubs.

Pugilism as art is the magnificent obsession of the advertising executive Marvin Sloves. His collection includes "anything you can think of that depicts boxing: paintings, ashtrays, punch bowls, walking sticks, umbrellas, porcelains, bronzes." For Jim Lehrer of television's "MacNeil/Lehrer Newshour," it's bus line paraphernalia—mostly signs, posters, and fixtures.

Collections centering on a particular animal are quite popular: frogs, bears, elephants, mice, and of course dogs and cats in every conceivable medium—porcelain, bronze, pewter, fabric, crystal, silver, gold, you name it. I have also run into hand collections—drawings of hands, paintings of hands, plaster casts of hands, photographs of hands. Howard and Helene Moore of Manhattan have 450 pieces in their collection, and every one depicts a kissing couple.

There are also lots of small subspecialties that attract loyal, sometimes fanatical followings. One may choose to collect all forms of English pottery, or one may choose to collect Wedgwood only. One fellow I know collects only English milk jugs made between 1800 and 1880. Paperweight collectors are a breed unto themselves, as are collectors of netsuke, Fiestaware, coin-operated machines, and so on. Each group has its own newsletters, holds its own conventions, and shares a sort of collective personality that makes it a unique and important part of the collecting world.

Zeroing in on a tiny subspecialty can reap gigantic rewards for the true connoisseur. Barbara Johnson, an attorney from Princeton, New Jersey, started collecting scrimshaw after she fell in love with these whalebone carvings while on an excursion to Cape Cod. When she decided to sell her collection and was looking for an auction house, it didn't hurt that we were born under the same astrological sign. I also offered to fill Sotheby's with baskets full of geraniums, her favorite flower, if she would consign the collection to us. She did, and those little decorated fragments of whalebone and ivory earned Mrs. Johnson more than $4 million.

Once you have chosen an area to collect in, do not feel constrained by its limits. There is no law that says once you have picked out a particular area you can't move on or expand. On the contrary, you would not be much of a collector if you didn't become a little fidgety. Inevitably, your tastes broaden and mature; they *evolve* to a higher plane.

In Barbara Johnson's case, as with John Gaines and all accomplished collectors, she waited until she found the particular type of object that captured her fancy. For whatever reason—the exquisite craftsmanship, the smooth texture of the ivory and bone, the haunting connection with the sea, or all of the above—scrimshaw clearly struck a chord with her.

Johnson assembled one of the world's great collections of scrimshaw because she identified with it. Therein lies an important lesson. If you don't have that gut feeling about something, there is no point in collecting it. Time and time again I have seen people start collecting abstract art or French antiques because they feel it is the thing to do—not because of any deeply felt appreciation of these objects. They almost always fail, and worst of all, they never have any fun at it because they have no feel for their collection.

The Cosby Effect

You cannot force anybody to become a connoisseur, but you most assuredly can help point them in the right direction. Bill Cosby is a veteran collector, and for years his enthusiasm for acquiring American antiques was as unbridled as his enthusiasm for making people laugh. Early in his collecting career, Bill came to me for advice. I told him what I tell all aspiring connoisseurs: before buying, educate yourself. Go to museums, talk to the experts, find out all you can about the field in general and the pieces that interest you in particular. From that point on Bill was more patient, more selective, more disciplined and purposeful —and in the process he became one of the finest collectors I've known.

One day I received a call from him asking if I would take part in an episode of "The Cosby Show." As fans of the series know, each episode has a message. Through the Huxtables, Bill wanted to give his huge audience some idea of how collecting can enrich a family's life as well as provide a valuable link to the past. One of the show's writers was dispatched to Sotheby's and followed me around, attending receptions and important sales as he gathered material. Paintings, antiques, carpets—even my auctioneer's podium—were shipped across town to the studio where "The Cosby Show" is taped.

The premise of the episode was rather straightforward: The Huxtables fall in love with a painting that turns out to have been the work of one of their ancestors. They are determined to have the painting hanging on their wall, but first they must buy it at an auction. Playing myself, I get to show the Huxtables how to go about it. Incidentally, many of those "props" that fill the Huxtables' New York town house are actually genuine paintings and antiques that clearly reflect the star's sophisticated tastes.

All in the Family: Couples Who Collect

As much as tennis or skiing, collecting is a sport perfectly suited to couples. Bill and Camille Cosby are a perfect example. So were the Duke and Duchess of Windsor, and Elizabeth Taylor and Richard Burton—two married couples who knew how to make the folks at Cartier and Harry Winston sit up and take notice.

In my experience, it is usually the woman who is the catalyst; she will bring her man around. But once the man gets drawn into the auction scene, he is likely to enjoy it even more than the woman does.

A perfect case in point is the midwestern girl who grew up in a house filled with weathered eighteenth-century furniture. When she married a young graduate school student in the late 1950s, she brought a half-dozen pieces along to fill up their small apartment. "That's all it was then," she recalls. "Just functional furniture that I felt comfortable with—a chest of drawers, a couple of drop-leaf tables, a wing chair. The whole batch had cost less than three thousand dollars."

Before long, she realized that the fine old Massachusetts furniture that cluttered their college apartment was far more than just "functional." There was, she explains, "something about mahogany that had been polished for a hundred and seventy years that spoke to me, something about the design that I could respond to." She soon became an avid collector, and her husband "just sort of fell into it." It was he, in fact, who in 1958 made their first purchase as bona fide collectors, shelling out $1,500 for a Rhode Island tea table.

As time went on, they built a business and raised a family— all the while pursuing their passion for American furniture. "We don't play golf, we don't play tennis, we don't travel to Europe, and we don't own a boat," she explains. "We just buy old wood."

THE ROAD TO CONNOISSEURSHIP

Their taste for "old wood" has evolved over the years. "I was nineteen when I started," she says, "so I should *hope* that I grew as a collector." From the unadorned Massachusetts pieces that she and her husband bought as college kids, they have stepped up to Philadelphia Chippendale and more elaborate Federal designs.

Their collection of American furniture is now one of the finest in the country and undoubtedly worth millions, but this couple does allow that they have a few regrets. "I have never regretted the things that I bid on," the midwestern girl explains, "only the things that I *didn't* bid on. But you can't buy everything." She also regrets the one time she made the decision to sell something from the family's collection. "It was only a pair of little wing chairs," she recalls, "but I knew it was a mistake the minute the gavel came down. I should have kept those chairs in the attic for my grandchildren."

Collecting couples bring a vitality and commitment with them that is often quite remarkable. Indeed, some of the greatest connoisseurs of all time have been husband and wife teams whose shared passion for a particular area has made them a formidable force in the marketplace. Where such collecting couples are concerned, the whole is usually a lot more than the sum of its parts.

Topping my personal list of favorite couples were Colonel Edgar Garbisch and his wife, the Chrysler heiress Bernice Garbisch. They knew my father well, but I really got to know Bernice Chrysler Garbisch through the American furniture sales at Sotheby's. She was a great collector of American furniture, and I was always haunting the exhibitions, so we kept bumping into each other.

The real turning point in our friendship came during my first year at Parke-Bernet. I was having lunch at the counter of Schrafft's when Bernice sat down next to me and ordered a sandwich. We chatted about our mutual love of Americana, and being a big sport (I was making all of $7,000 a year then), I picked up her check. Later, I asked my father if that was an allowable charge to the company. It was, and it became my very first expense account charge.

Colonel Garbisch, who had been an all-American football player in his youth, was the prototypical man's man—big, raw-boned, and gregarious. We were both incorrigible golf enthusiasts, and we often made the same bet—a single dollar bill, signed by the loser and suitable for framing. The interests that we had in sports as well as in collecting became the anchor of a twenty-year friendship.

The Garbisches were one of the closest couples I have ever seen. College sweethearts, they did everything together, and they ended each day by taking a cup of warm milk up to bed and sharing it. When it came to collecting, they went to exhibitions together and picked out the paintings and the furniture together. And although she was a woman of real means, Bernice always deferred to her husband as the Man in Charge. He made all the decisions, but only after consulting her. The Garbisches were a package deal; it was impossible to think of one without the other. Fittingly, they died within hours of each other, on December 26, 1979.

On many occasions, we discussed how their estate might be sold, and those instructions were put into a letter between us and attached to the Garbisches' will. We held the sale under a tent at their Pokety Farms estate, and I felt grateful to be able to fulfill their final wishes concerning the manner in which their art treasures would be sold. The Garbisch collection, which was actually dispersed in two sales, included magnificent French antiques, European porcelains, and the works of Impressionist and Modern masters.

The Garbisches were not alone in turning a his-and-her married pastime into one of the world's great collections. Jack and Belle Linksy, the Staple King and his bride, also shared everything—including a streak of impatience. One day, Belle Linksy was spotted trying to buy a huge Franz Kline canvas right off the sidewalk as it was being carried into a Fifty-seventh Street gallery in New York. Another time it was a huge Jackson Pollock being lifted off a truck. In both cases, she had to wait until the gallery shows, of course. But she got the paintings in the end.

Jack Linsky was cut from the same cloth. On one occasion I looked out my office window and saw Jack struggling to angle something into the back seat of a cab. It was the Louis XV oak and mahogany veneered marquetry table that once belonged to Madame de Pompadour. The Linksys had just purchased the table from the estate of Martha Baird Rockefeller for $410,000. Jack just couldn't wait to get their newest acquisition home.

Both husband and wife had a tremendous intellectual curiosity. They had an extensive art library in their home and made routine pilgrimages to Europe in search of new quarry. Their collective eye was phenomenal. Without hesitating, they could tell that a bronze that appeared to be from the fifteenth century was actually a perfect copy of a fifteenth-century work executed two hundred years later, or they could reel off in detail the provenance of a Louis XIV settee. It is hard to imagine that a day went by without the two thinking about ways to add to their collection.

One day an official of a major museum dropped by and scoffed at their Fabergé eggs. He urged the Linskys to sell them, and they did. For years afterward, as Malcolm Forbes bid millions for egg after egg, Belle would shake her head. "I never," she would mutter in exasperation, "should have sold those damn eggs." That was the last time the Linskys ignored their own instincts.

But even without the Fabergé eggs, the Linskys left a mind-boggling legacy of old masters, French furniture, and sculpture —some of which are housed in their own gallery at the Metropolitan Museum. Like all great collecting couples, they fanned the fires of each other's desire to acquire.

The Specialists

On an art-buying budget nowhere near that of either the Garbisches or the Linskys, Victor and Sally Ganz managed to build one of the finest contemporary collections in the world by zeroing in on a half-dozen artists.

The first half of the Ganzes' collecting career was devoted to one well-chosen master. "Victor started very early," Sally Ganz recalls of her husband, a costume jeweler who died in 1987 at the age of seventy-four. "When he was still a teenager, he bought a few drawings and paintings. Even then, he had the most incredible eye.

"From the start of our marriage, we spent every weekend looking at art," says Sally. "On one of those weekend excursions in 1941, we spotted a glorious Picasso in a gallery window and instantly fell in love with it." The Ganzes bought *The Dream* for a few hundred dollars. "It was terribly expensive for us at the time," says Sally, "and most of our friends thought it was sort of a bizarre and daring thing to do." Victor Ganz stuck with this one artist, accumulating only what he considered to be the finest examples of Picasso's work that fell within his budget, for twenty years. "We could appreciate Klee and the others, but there was something very, very special about Picasso. We were convinced early on that he was *the* twentieth-century master, but more importantly, it was as if his paintings spoke directly to us."

By the early 1960s, the Ganzes found themselves priced out of the market for Picassos. "We just couldn't afford him anymore," says Sally. So they turned to the new breed of young contemporary artists who would come to dominate the New York art scene. True to form, Victor Ganz selected the work of only four of these artists—Jasper Johns, Robert Rauschenberg, Frank Stella, and Eva Hesse—to add to his remarkable, museum-quality collection.

THE ROAD TO CONNOISSEURSHIP

There was an added dividend to collecting as-yet-undiscovered artists. "When artists know you are acquiring their work out of love and not as an investment," explains Sally, "they want to know you as much as you want to know them."

While Victor was surely the driving force here, Sally shared in his splendid addiction. Both Ganzes had a unique eye for pictures that were often devoid of color and for stark sculptures that were, in the words of one observer, "nearly always difficult and rebarbative and secretive and ironic." Their collection was quirky, idiosyncratic, provocative, daring—in a word, brilliant.

When I had the pleasure of auctioning the Ganz collection in November of 1988, none of us were prepared for the furor the twelve lots by four modern masters were to ignite. By the end of the evening, the dozen works had brought a total of more than $41 million.

Even so, for Victor and Sally Ganz the personal rewards far outweighed the financial ones. During forty-five years as collectors, the Ganzes created an environment that allowed the couple to totally immerse themselves in their art without becoming slaves to it. Their home was neither a museum nor a shrine; the Ganzes were just as interested in displaying family photographs as their Picassos. "I like the way the Ganzes do it," said Jasper Johns. "I like the way they put the table lamps in front of the pictures."

"We never bought art strictly as an investment," says Sally. "Of course it turned out to be the greatest investment of our lives." As for the dozen pictures that made up the landmark Sotheby's sale, Sally Ganz allows that she did not want to part with them. It was, however, the only practical way to settle her late husband's estate. "It was heartbreaking, but those paintings will go on to have other lives. Besides, I have plenty more left over...."

Fran Stark, along with her husband, Ray, is one of Hollywood's leading connoisseurs of modern art. She may have inherited her particular passion for art from her mother, the legendary comedienne Fannie Brice, who was both a part-time painter and a collector. But Fran's brother William, who later took up painting himself, was ahead of his sister. "Billy is very knowledgeable," Fran has said. "He bought a Picasso when he was eleven years old. I bought a show horse at the same age, and it's long since gone to the glue factory. Billy still has his Picasso."

The film producer Ray Stark denies that he and Fran are collectors. They merely, he insists, like to surround themselves with objects that are beautiful and soothing—"things we want to live with."

For him, it is sculpture. "Painting is fine," he has said, "but sculpture you can actually touch, and...I love the sensuousness." Their red brick Georgian-style Beverly Hills house, formerly the home of Humphrey Bogart, boasts a sculpture garden chockablock with Aristide Maillol, René Magritte, and Moore.

Ironically, Stark fell into collecting sculpture quite by accident. During a party at the home of Joe Hirshhorn, he offhandedly complimented his host on one of his statues, *Figure for Landscape* by Barbara Hepworth. A few days later, a Hepworth was delivered to Stark's door, courtesy of Hirshhorn.

Stark really embraced his newfound hobby after he met Henry Moore in London. The two became fast friends, and soon Moore's mammoth works were being shipped to the Starks' California home, sometimes two at a time. From that starting point, Stark expanded his collection to include bronzes by Rodin, Renoir, and Giacometti.

While her husband scouted galleries and auction houses for sculpture to suit his tastes for the sensuous, Fran Stark picked up where her famous mother left off as a connoisseur of paintings. Starting with a Rouault purchased in 1958, she amassed a collection that blends with Ray's taste in the three-dimensional: beguiling works by Chagall, Monet, Braque, Picasso, and Max Pechstein, among others. In addition, there are Calders on the tabletops and Léger-designed carpets on the floors.

No collecting couple has had a greater impact on contemporary art than Robert and Ethel Scull. The Sculls, who owned a New York taxi fleet, actually set out to collect Renaissance bronzes and Impressionists. But when their first painting—a Utrillo that Bob bought for $245—turned out to be a fake, they went out and bought a Jasper Johns.

After building a formidable collection of such Abstract Expressionists as Mark Rothko, Franz Kline, and Willem de Kooning, Ethel discovered a young artist named Andy Warhol. That very day, she spent $1,400 on four Warhol canvases, including a couple of Campbell's soup cans. The Sculls' marriage ended bitterly, but their collection stood the test of time. In two sales in the late 1980s, just two of the Jasper Johns works they had purchased in the early 1960s for a few thousand dollars brought a combined price of nearly $30 million.

The Shoestring Collector

Their taxi empire supplied Robert and Ethel Scull with the means to pursue their passion for art, but they didn't really need a fortune. Most of their early purchases were made with a few thousand or even a few hundred dollars. The fact of the matter is that even today you can collect quality on a modest budget. Combining her income as a New York City librarian with his postal worker's pension, Dorothy and Herbert Vogel quietly assembled a first-rate collection of Minimalist and Conceptual art —some 1,500 works by such acclaimed artists as Carl André, Robert Mangold, and Christo.

The Vogels came to collecting rather late. In his mid-thirties, after having been indifferent toward art, Herbert was inexplicably bitten by the bug. He started working night shifts at the post office so he could take art classes during the day. Dorothy, in the meantime, went along for the ride. The first piece the Vogels bought together was a miniature crushed automobile sculpture

THE BEST OF EVERYTHING

by John Chamberlain, which they later lent to the Guggenheim Museum.

Their collection was worth a not-so-small fortune by the 1980s, partly because the Vogels held on to every piece they bought. "Collecting has sort of taken over our lives," conceded Dorothy, who during the same twenty-year period collected bookmarks and shopping bags. "When you find something, you just know it. You say, 'I want it.' It's like a high. It's like falling in love." When it came to choosing names for their seven cats, the Vogels went mainstream: Renoir, Cézanne, Corot, Manet, Picasso, Whistler, and Tiffany.

Developing
Your Eye

Make no mistake about it. If you want to become a connoisseur, you are going to have to invest your time and your energy in the process. You must train your eye to increasing levels of artistic and aesthetic sophistication. This means exposing yourself to all that is available. In essence, then, connoisseurship is the ultimate in self-education: you establish the curriculum, you choose the study materials, you determine the depth of learning you wish to pursue, and you learn at your own pace.

Collecting, of course, is what puts teeth into the process. There is nothing like spending money—putting your expertise and your cash on the line—to concentrate the mind.

Here are four avenues toward your education as a connoisseur.

Reading and Research

Today there are countless magazines and newspapers specifically for and about the art world. At one end of the spectrum there are the more scholarly periodicals, such as *Apollo, Artforum, Art in America, Antiques World, The Magazine Antiques,* and *Art News.* For harder market information, there are *Art & Antiques, Art & Auction, Connoisseur,* the *Maine Antiques Digest, Art Newsletter,* and *The Newtown Bee.* Auction house newsletters (we publish ours ten times a year) offer highlights of the season and reviews of recent auctions worldwide.

The shelves of most bookstores are heaped with art reference works, ranging from survey books such as H. W. Janson's to volumes that deal with a specific collecting category—dolls, say, or musical instruments. Sotheby's own publications range from our annual *Sotheby's Art at Auction* and *International Price Guide* to such specific topics as *Drawing Instruments, 1580–1980, Sherry and the Sherry Bodegas, Early Netherlandish Painting: The Thyssen-Bornemisza Collection,* and *Automata: The Golden Age, 1848–1914.*

One of the best ways to learn a lot in a relatively short amount of time, and to find collecting opportunities in every price range, is to subscribe to auction house catalogues. Each catalogue, assembled by in-house experts, blends scholarly knowledge with authoritative market information (those all-important price estimates, for example). Regardless of the area you have chosen, catalogue subscriptions give you a jump on the competition, allowing you to preview hundreds of works of art coming up for sale—from, as we say, "the rarest masterworks to some surprisingly affordable discoveries."

Sotheby's publishes more than 120 catalogues a year in the United States. Our nineteenth-century European paintings and drawings catalogue, for example, includes the French Barbizon school and the Salon painters as well as their English, Continental, and Scandinavian contemporaries. Our fine books and manuscripts catalogues provide a sense of the evolution of thought in a wide range of fields, from the illuminated manuscripts of the Middle Ages to first editions by James Joyce and D. H. Lawrence. Sotheby's postage stamp catalogue traces the history of philately from the first stamps issued in England in 1840 to the special issues of the twentieth century. The wine catalogue covers more than just the rarest wines of Europe; it also includes cigars and related items. How about Nepalese and Tibetan bronzes? Movie memorabilia? Or maybe Chinese snuff bottles? The auction house catalogues cover them all, providing the collector with a primer on auction house lingo, descriptive catalogue phraseology, price ranges, and so forth. As far as printed resources are concerned, none are of more value in educating the collector's eye than the auction house catalogues. They give you, in a nutshell, a standard for comparison.

Consulting

Many newcomers are surprised to discover how accessible art experts and other professionals in the collecting world really are. Most are flattered to be asked. Think about how animated you become about your own line of work when someone seems truly interested in what you do. At Sotheby's alone, our two hundred specialists in more than seventy different collecting categories are paid to a large extent to answer your questions.

The experienced and reputable dealer should not be overlooked as a valuable source of information. After all, a dealer is very knowledgeable about everything that goes on in his collecting field because the very nature of his business is to invest in that field. What he doesn't know can hurt him, so he keeps abreast not only of broad trends in the market but of all the late-breaking news regarding upcoming auction sales.

The Joseph Duveens have their counterparts in today's market. Since you represent a potential customer to them, they are invariably eager to answer any questions you may have about the area in which they specialize.

Perhaps the most frequently overlooked resource tool in the individual collector's quest for knowledge is the museum curator. We tend to forget that museums are public institutions, there to serve the public's cultural good. Many people are intimidated by the grand edifices and the masterpieces. Even when the museum is small and run by the local historical society, the average person is reluctant to "bother" museum officials with inquiries. Remember that a primary function of any museum is education, and no curator worth his salt will hesitate to help you find the answers to your questions.

Networking

There are countless societies, seminars, field trips, and conferences relating to specific collecting areas. Groups of collectors are always looking for others with whom to share their passion.

As might be expected, there are organizations for Early American antiques collectors, print collectors, Oriental art collectors, Art Nouveau/Art Deco collectors, Western art collectors, doll collectors, antiquities collectors, and so on. But did you know that there are also dozens of match cover clubs (people who collect matchbook covers call themselves "phillumenists") or that fifteen thousand people belong to the Beer Can Collectors of America?

It doesn't stop there. There is also an International Club for

Collectors of Hatpins and Hatpin Holders, a Metropolitan Post-card Club, an American Lock Collectors' Association, a Paper-weight Collectors' Association, a National Depression Glass Association, a Marble Collectors Society of America, a Society for the Collectors of Brand-Name Pencils, an American Society of Military Insignia Collectors, a Tin Container Collectors Association, and a group that calls itself the Spark Plug Collectors of America.

If you collect, there is an organization out there for you. One of the simplest ways to locate it is to visit your local library, where you will probably find it listed in the Gale Research Company's annual *Encyclopedia of Associations*.

Just as important are the informal contacts you will make by rubbing shoulders with other dedicated souls in your chosen area. Wherever I go in the country, I tend to see many of the same eager faces at museum exhibitions, gallery openings, and auctions. These people, all constantly seeking out information and refining their tastes, have formed a sort of unofficial network that gives them the answers they need. With each passing year, those faces grow younger and younger as more people under the age of fifty realize that there are more pleasurable ways of investing their capital than buying CDs.

One friend of mine, a fellow collector of American furniture, feels this network is not only broadening but "an awful lot of fun. You can be in a strange city, go straight to the nearest museum or antiques shop, and find a kindred spirit, someone who shares your passion for collecting, an immediate friend. My husband and I don't have to join a country club. We meet plenty of marvelous people just through collecting."

Do not isolate yourself. Tap into the collecting world's gossip network, and you will be able to spot trends as they develop.

Participation

Get out and start looking. Browse. Attend exhibitions. Immerse yourself in this world and you will be amazed how much you will be able to pick up just through osmosis.

Once again, the auction house specifically encourages participation to the limit. The wonderful "please touch" policy that all but pleads with you to handle the merchandise cannot be matched anywhere else. Nor will you find any more accurate barometer for the art and antiques market than an auction house salesroom. So if you can visit an auction house, by all means do so.

Over and above what the curators can tell you, museums offer all sorts of special courses and programs. I owe a great deal to one such course, a series of postgraduate lectures in decorative arts offered by Columbia University and given in the evenings at the Metropolitan Museum in New York.

Even as a professional, these classes, which I took shortly after starting my auction career, were of tremendous help to me in categorizing the European decorative arts of the eighteenth century—everything from furniture to silver to porcelain, with a dash of architecture tossed in for good measure. This area is easily the most widely collected, and with good reason. Eighteenth-century Europe is the epoch that is most revered by connoisseurs of the decorative arts—a time when, most experts agree, craftsmanship reached its zenith.

The six-week course, which was taught by Carl Dautterman, one of the Met's most revered curators, took us on a marvelous walking tour of the eighteenth century. We were given the opportunity to study treasured antiques of the time up close, and to compare them to the designs of other eras. We also got to look at some pretty diabolically clever fakes. Even museums get saddled with one now and again.

DEVELOPING YOUR EYE

This class brought me to the realization that the decorative arts are in essence an extension of architecture, and that architecture in turn reflects the mood of the times. I discovered that a design line can be followed from the architecture of a Georgian house down to the design of the dining-room table and of the utensils and the plates. A Louis XVI chair could be looked upon as a work of architecture, I discovered to my surprise, and a house as a work of art.

It may sound odd that someone who had been exposed to these objects his entire life would need a course to open his eyes to this rather essential connection between architecture and the decorative arts. But these classes provided me the one thing I had been lacking: a frame of reference, a grid to help me make sense of it all. (The tables were turned years later when, as an adviser to collectors, my former teacher would come to Sotheby's and bid on his clients' behalf.)

Self-education is the hallmark of the connoisseur. The more you understand the things you collect, the more you can appreciate them. The more you appreciate these objects, the more they will talk to you and become a part of your life.

Ultimately, of course, all this reading and research and consulting and course-taking and exhibition-watching is leading you straight to that moment when you take the plunge. Why not just give a dealer or some other expert the money and have him invest it for you? "I think discovery is one of the great joys of collecting," answers Dorothy Rodgers, the widow of the great composer Richard Rodgers and an established modern art collector in her own right. "I wouldn't delegate that pleasure to anyone else, even if he were to offer me a free Picasso with every third purchase."

Discovery is indeed one of the important and satisfying elements of collecting. So are knowledge and commitment. Look at collecting in much the same way you look at your career and your personal relationships. Commit yourself wholeheartedly to the process. Do not go off like a unguided missile. Before you invest a dime, invest your *time* in finding out all that you can about your chosen area of collecting.

With a little guidance and a lot of passion, you will make sound investments in beautiful objects—whether your chosen hunting ground is a gallery, an antiques store, a flea market, or an auction house. You will also find, as William Paley, the Linskys, and other great connoisseurs have found, that no matter how big your eventual profit, the real payoff of collecting isn't monetary at all.

CHAPTER — SEVEN

The

Artful

Collector

• •

"Collecting is like education," Malcolm Forbes once observed. "There is an unending horizon if you really get turned on." Unfortunately, the vast majority of people who get turned on to collecting—the millions who buy art books, go to museums, and browse through antiques shops and art galleries—fail to take that extra step and become directly involved. Convinced that collecting is still strictly a game for the very rich, they resign themselves to the role of spectator.

What strikes me as particularly sad is that these are the very people who stand to gain the most from getting involved. Unlike some of the rich "pointers" who merely point at something and buy it without any aesthetic sensibility, they have already done their homework. They not only know what they like, they know *why* they like it. Yet they are fearful of taking that first step.

There is an art to collecting, and for the true collector as well as the true artist there are no real shortcuts. There are, nevertheless, a few strategies that will help you avoid some of the pitfalls on your journey to connoisseurship. The first step is not only quite painless, it is downright enjoyable.

Go Out and Buy Something

You can't hang cash or a share of IBM on your wall, and there comes a time when all individuals seek that "something more" to enhance their lives. These people already have the houses and the boats, and when they see a Picasso drawing or a Remington bronze at a friend's house, they immediately think to themselves: "Now *that's* what I should have."

So they run out to a gallery and buy something expensive (always a "name" work of art, something recognizable). The next thing that happens I have witnessed so many times I am now convinced it must be peculiar to our national character. The impulsive buyer wakes up and thinks, "My God, here I am a reasonably intelligent, prudent businessman and I just laid out thousands of dollars to buy something that I don't know a damn thing about."

Soon he is going to museums and galleries and auction houses, speaking with dealers and experts—desperately finding out all that he can about his new investment. *That* is how he becomes a bona fide collector.

In my own case, it was not until I'd gotten up the nerve to buy that small lot of antiquities that I became serious about ancient cultures. The same is true of my interest in American furniture, which really took off only after I'd purchased a chest of drawers for a few hundred dollars.

I see it over and over again: *Americans have to spend their money before you can get their attention.* So if you are a little ambivalent about collecting or uncertain about what it is you want to collect, take that initial plunge and see how you feel about it. I am not suggesting that you buy something just for the sake of it. Well, not entirely, anyway.

If you require a little nudge, go out and create a reason to collect. In writing about ways to "adopt" an antique, the journalist Bob Arehart has told of how he built a collection around his astrological sign. Arehart is a Leo, so it seemed only logical that he would start hunting for leonine images. One favorite is a French bronze lion Arehart says he "discovered on a trip to London and carried home on my lap in the airplane. In Chicago I found silver lion knife holders. On another excursion I discovered a real treasure: a carved teakwood lioness and cub with ivory teeth, probably early English."

Collecting is a lot like riding a bicycle; you need training wheels until you get your balance. Once something has caught your fancy, you should ask a lot of questions before you pull out your wallet. But the fact remains that, until you actually make that first purchase, any reading, research, and museum-browsing you do is really little more than an academic exercise. Once you've put your money down, that's when you will begin to experience the strong feelings that are the hallmark of a real collector.

Every Generation Creates Its Own Nostalgia

While it is obvious that we all connect in some way with ancient civilizations and that the French Impressionists strike a universal emotional chord, many people collect strictly for reasons of nostalgia. They see a part of their own past that evokes fond memories and they want that tangible reminder of the past. This, in fact, is what creates a market—a group of people vying for the same reminders of a shared past or a common cultural heritage.

Nostalgic appeal often has absolutely nothing to do with our own past. We can be nostalgic for another era as well. I am convinced that the current rage for American furniture is a by-product of the whole pride-in America sentiment that has swept the country in recent years. The same is true of Western art, which harkens back to the rough-and-ready days of the cowboys, and of Norman Rockwell's all-American *Saturday Evening Post* paintings, which can now fetch six-figure sums.

Indeed, all forms of Americana, from Currier & Ives prints and Shaker furniture to weather vanes and samplers, stir a desire in many of us for a return to a simpler time. The Good Old Days. I once met a collector who so immersed himself in eighteenth-century art and antiques that his house was lighted entirely by candles.

Connoisseurs of movie memorabilia, many of whom were born years after such classics as *Citizen Kane* and *Casablanca* were made, constitute another example of collecting out of one's own time. A number of items, such as the Rosebud sled and Dorothy's ruby slippers, are out of reach of most novice collectors. But posters, annotated scripts, props, and other historic Hollywood paraphernalia offer wonderful opportunities for the diehard movie buff.

Hollywood costumes, for example, can range in price from $22,000 for Judy Garland's cotton blue and white dress from *The Wizard of Oz* and $16,500 for Vivien Leigh's two-piece cotton day dress from *Gone With the Wind* to $2,530 for the two-piece gray outfit worn by Julie Andrews in *The Sound of Music,* $2,650 for Marilyn Monroe's silk pajamas from *The Seven Year Itch,* and $1,320 for one of Judy Garland's dancing costumes from *The Easter Parade.*

It is the form of nostalgia that each generation in effect creates for itself that offers new and exciting opportunities to novice collectors. There is no better example of this than Disneyana. I once visited our Los Angeles galleries to auction off some Walt Disney memorabilia. The entire auction brought $15,000— hardly worth doing by Sotheby's standards. More than fifteen years later, that same auction would probably earn in the neighborhood of $200,000.

Baby boomers, who grew up on such Disney animated classics as *Pinocchio, Dumbo, Bambi, Peter Pan,* and *The Lady and the Tramp,* devotedly collect the hand-painted celluloids used to make the films. These "cels," as they are called, can bring anywhere between $700 and $15,000, depending largely on the rarity of the frame. The original watercolor backgrounds against which many of the cels were shot are far fewer in number, and therefore even more keenly sought by collectors. A watercolor background might command as much as $30,000. Our 1989 sale of 560 cels from *Who Framed Roger Rabbit?* brought $1.7 million —quite a lot for a film that was then barely a year old.

Of course, Disneymania does not stop there. There are the famous (and now quite costly) Mickey Mouse watches, and a whole array of toys from the 1940s and 1950s. In 1988, a Japanese-made plastic figure of Mickey Mouse riding Pluto sold for $6,600. A Donald Duck carousel brought $5,500, while another Japanese toy, a Mickey that walked, sold for $4,400.

The impact of baby boomers also extends to rock-and-roll memorabilia, comic books, classic automobiles from the fifties, and Howdy Doody dolls—in short, anything that conjures up life during the Eisenhower era.

People in this same age group also vie for icons of the psychedelic sixties. More rock memorabilia, of course, but also genuine art. No artist is more closely identified with that turbulent time than Peter Max, who was catapulted to prominence as a leading exponent of psychedelic art. Since the mid-1970s, however, Max's work has remained well within reach of the mid-level collector. As recently as 1984, a Peter Max painting of a reclining nude sold for around $4,000. Today, the same painting fetches $20,000—a strong indication of where the market is headed as more and more people in their forties and under with means begin to collect seriously.

The real trick is to anticipate what collectibles will ride in on the next wave of nostalgia—not the ephemera of a generation but the objects which conjure up such a depth of emotion that they will have true and lasting value.

Be Greedy on Your Own Behalf

Remember, you aren't spending money when you collect. You are merely converting your assets into a more pleasurable form. A connoisseur should operate within a budget, so long as that budget is flexible enough to satisfy the collector's passion.

It bears repeating that you should resist getting caught up in auction fever. You should know how high you are willing to bid at auction, and you should try to stick to your self-imposed limit. Yet one of the biggest mistakes newcomers make is to pass up opportunities because they fear going a bit over the budget they have set for an acquisition.

Trouble also arises when people set that limit at an unrealistically low level, effectively removing themselves as serious contenders even before bidding has begun (or, if you are buying from a dealer, before you've set foot in his shop).

When buying at auction, be prepared to spend within the estimate. If you're lucky enough to land a bargain, fine. But if the bidding exceeds the maximum, keep in mind that a good part of the joy of collecting is in the hunt, the thrill of the chase. If you have set a limit of $2,000, and that other fellow is willing to go to $2,100, now is not the time to get cold feet. Pay the extra $200 if that is what it takes to own that object you truly want.

Risky? Not at all. Even though you ended up spending a little more than you originally intended, the object in question should increase its value with time. Invest that little extra now, and you will find those same collectors ready to pay a much higher price when you decide to sell it down the road. The bid most regretted is the one not made.

Buy the Best You Can Buy

With inflation, everything goes up; during a recession, the best still goes up. While $50,000 won't buy you much of an Impressionist painting, it can nonetheless buy something quite spectacular. A painting from the twentieth-century school of Paris, perhaps. An old master drawing or a splendid piece of American furniture.

Instead of minor works by major artists and craftsmen, you would do better to seek out major works by lesser artists and craftsmen. Truly dedicated collectors are always willing to pay whatever it takes to obtain perfection in their chosen category, but they have a special disdain for the inferior. At all costs, you want to avoid that no-man's-land between mediocre works by first-rate artists and first-rate works by secondary artists.

If your passion is Chinese porcelain, but the best examples of early Ming are beyond your reach, there are still affordable pieces that represent the best of the Guangxu and Qianlong periods. You could spend upward of $25,000 for one of Frederic Remington's lesser bronzes or less than half that for the very best work of Cyrus Edwin Dallin, Charles H. Humphries, and a score of other Western sculptors. Rather than investing a small fortune in a marginal Rothko, take the time to investigate the scores of first-rate contemporary artists whose finest efforts still fall into the low five figures.

One of the many colorful characters I've encountered in my years at Sotheby's was Abraham Braun. Abe started out with a pushcart on the streets of Chicago collecting used bottles during the Depression and wound up supplying the major breweries.

*A Wucai jar and cover, circa 1750; not an
Imperial piece but at $2,090 a first-rate example
of Chinese quality and craftsmanship*

As it happened, Abe also had a marvelous eye for American furniture and Mexican art. In the course of one sale, I turned to him and asked why he hadn't bid on a rather attractive piece of Federal furniture. He shrugged and said, "It's a gin and tonic."

"What do you mean?"

"You know," he said, "a *gin and tonic*. Something you order when you don't really like to drink but want to sound like you do."

It was his way of saying that, even though it was a fine piece, it had failed to move him. It didn't live up to his standards. Don't settle for just another gin and tonic. Buy the best that you can buy.

The Ways of the Contrarian

Contrarian buying—simply going against the grain—has worked for a number of collectors. It is predicated on the painfully logical assumption that you'll get the best prices for things fewer people seem to want. Since virtually every area of collecting eventually has its day, all you have to do is buy the best you can and then sit tight. How else are you going to "buy low, sell high"?

This strategy has worked spectacularly for Malcolm Forbes, who has always followed the advice of one man: himself.

It was on a trip to London one Easter in the early 1960s that Malcolm spotted a Fabergé egg in a shopwindow and bought it for his wife. Soon he was hooked on these chimerical creations designed by Peter Carl Fabergé for the Russian imperial court. Most collectors thought the egg fancier in their midst was, well, cracked.

All of which was perfectly fine with Malcolm, who had the field largely to himself until 1965. That year I was presiding at the podium when Malcolm got into a heated bidding war with Alexander Schaffer, the owner of New York's À la Vieille Russie and the major dealer in Russian works of art. To win it, Malcolm had to put up $50,000—quite an astounding figure for the time. Realizing that his opponent would pay whatever it took to add another egg to his collection, Schaffer then began bringing the eggs to Malcolm and, when necessary, bidding on his behalf.

In 1986, Malcolm Forbes bought his eleventh egg, for $1,760,000. "The score," announced the auctioneer, "is Forbes eleven–Russians ten." Later, Sotheby's made it an even dozen, putting Malcolm two up on the Kremlin.

As a collector of Fabergé, Malcolm has by no means confined himself to imperial eggs; he has also assembled a dazzling array of Fabergé watches, clocks, picture frames, boxes, animals, and other decorative objects. But by zeroing in on Fabergé eggs and committing himself to them at a time when they were considered declassé (remember the bad advice Belle Linksy got), the astute Mr. Forbes managed to pick up quite a few marvelous objects—including a number that had been sold by the Linskys—before the market caught fire.

Forbes's contrarian ways extended to American paintings (he started out in the early 1960s buying lesser-known contemporary neo-realists, such as Edward Melcarth and Walter Stuempfig) and to American autograph material, particularly presidential signatures. Forbes first became interested in autographs as a young man working in his father's office. "I thought 'autograph' meant just that," recalls Forbes, "so whenever a letter came into the office from somebody famous like J. P. Morgan or Henry Ford, I just cut out the signature, pasted it in a book, and threw the rest of the letter away! I guess collecting historic letters and documents is my way of atoning for that vandalism."

Even when he began collecting autographs in earnest, many people looked at Malcolm as something of a curiosity for spending thousands on items like Paul Revere's midnight ride expense report. These proved to be some of his shrewdest purchases, but there is still plenty of top-quality material out there. "This area remains a potential gold mine for collectors," says Forbes. "A letter can be so revealing, full of color and anecdotes—it can tell you so much more about a person than any artist's rendering. Compared to other areas, autograph material is vastly under-priced."

Another unlikely contrarian is Allen Funt, the host of television's "Candid Camera." Funt collected Pre-Raphaelite paintings in the early 1970s, when that particular school was at its nadir. The fact that these Victorian-era paintings were considered at best unfashionable and at worst blatantly tasteless mattered not at all to Funt, who had a particular affinity for the work of the Pre-Raphaelite painter Lawrence Alma-Tadema.

Within three years, Alma-Tadema and the rest of the Victorians were back in vogue. Funt's collection was worth more than twice what he had initially invested in it.

Not every contrarian has been so fortunate. Huntington Hartford became famous for his Midas touch in reverse. Relying principally on his instincts, Hartford assembled his own collection of Pre-Raphaelite paintings. Financial pressures forced him to sell at a loss in the early 1970s. Had he been able to hold on to those works just a few years longer, Hartford would have made millions on his original investment.

Still, there are plenty of times when it pays to march to a different drummer. Just make sure you have done your homework, weighed the variables, and assessed the risk. Don't collect something simply because it is out of favor and you think it will make a comeback. Collect it because it speaks to you. If it doesn't, you might as well invest in pork bellies.

The Suction Factor

It is an immutable law of physics: Nature abhors a vacuum. So it is in the world of collecting. As the most outstanding examples of a particular collecting category disappear from the market, something comes along to take their place.

The second-tier artists invariably jump in to fill the breach. The work of the Impressionists Gustave Caillebotte and Eugène Boudin, for example, sold for five figures three years ago. Now their paintings have jumped into the middle six-figure range. The same is true across the board, in every field, from paperweights and folk art to antiquities and photographs.

Just as often, however, the meteoric rise of one category of collecting can boost the fortunes of another. When Anthony Van Dyck, Rubens, and other old masters virtually disappeared from the market, collectors turned to Renoir, Monet, and van Gogh. Now that the crème de la crème of Impressionism and Post-Impressionism has begun to go the way of the old masters, many who would otherwise be collecting Rembrandt or Degas have shifted to twentieth-century modern and contemporary artists. Particularly strong are turn-of-the-century American artists, many of whose paintings are still available for a few thousand dollars. The best of these have begun to hit the high five- and the low six-figure levels.

The escalation in the 1960s and 1970s of prices for eighteenth-century Queen Anne and Chippendale pulled Federal furniture up from the second to the first tier. Now the best opportunities can be found in the area of late-nineteenth-century classical furniture. Since the best examples of Chinese ceramics can now cost as much as a Renoir, collectors have found a satisfying alternative in Chinese porcelain of a more recent vintage. Fans of Art Nouveau have turned out of necessity to Art Deco and, increasingly, to Art Moderne.

On the strength of a single name, the whole "suction" process can be greatly accelerated. The market for American bronze sculptures was moribund until the Geraldine Rockefeller Dodge sale in 1975. Under a tent on the grounds of Giralda, her vast New Jersey estate, I presided over the auction that revived interest in nineteenth- and twentieth-century American bronzes overnight. Records were broken as bidders vied for sculptures by Augustus Saint-Gaudens, Charles Russell, Charles H. Humphries, and Cyrus Edwin Dallin.

The popular Mrs. Dodge, a dog breeder as well as a respected collector and philanthropist, also owned sixty-eight works by the nineteenth-century animal painters Edwin Henry Landseer and Rosa Bonheur. These artists, long ridiculed by scholars and ignored by serious collectors, were suddenly back in vogue.

The suction factor guarantees that, for the collector who despairs of soaring prices, there will always be a sliver of light on the horizon. Go to that light. Buy something of superior quality from the second tier well *before* the first tier skyrockets out of sight.

Don't Be Scared Off by the Big Guys

By now, you may be feeling a tad intimidated by the power of certain monied groups to stand the art market on its head overnight. People who have quietly collected Art Nouveau for years cannot compete with a recording star willing to pay $50,000 or more for a Tiffany lamp.

No, you cannot hope to compete with the big spenders. Or can you? Time and time again I have seen people psych themselves out of the game when they could have walked away with the prize.

The standard scenario: A piece you would love to own is about to come up for sale, but you know that a half-dozen collectors with pockets deeper than yours want it as badly as you do. You will go to the auction, but you won't bother to examine the object closely or do your homework. What's the point? You won't get a fair shot at it anyway.

The day of the auction rolls around. Unbeknownst to you, two of the big spenders aren't there because they've got the flu,

two more couldn't make it because of unexpected business con-
flicts, and one spotted something he liked better in a gallery
window on the way to the sale and bought it instead. Yet another
key player simply forgot about the auction altogether.

So there you sit, along with a roomful of others who allowed
themselves to be intimidated by big money, staring in stunned
silence. Why, you wonder, is this lot failing to make even the
minimum estimate? Perhaps it really isn't the great piece you
thought it was, but there is no way to be certain since you never
did your homework. You sit there, powerless to act, while someone who had the presence of mind to come prepared nabs the
prize.

Don't allow yourself to be intimidated. Don't second-guess
the outcome of an auction. The action can take too many bizarre
twists and turns before the hammer comes down. Don't count
yourself out of the running prematurely. In the auction game, as
in baseball, it ain't over till it's over. Even if you are not successful
your first time out, you will be a smarter collector for the experience.

Let Us Appraise the Appraisers

Any smart collector should know what his property is worth. Not
only should you have a collectible appraised as soon as you bring
it home, you should have it reappraised every three years just to
keep abreast of the market. Why? Primarily to make sure that you
have sufficient insurance, but also to determine the fair market
value should you decide to sell or to swap with another collector.
You may also need to know, for works that are either gifts or
bequests, how much you owe the IRS in gift or estate taxes.

It is nothing short of frightening to see who claims to be a
qualified appraiser these days. In late 1988, we received an appraisal for an estate in Arkansas that not only misspelled the
names of artists but misidentified them altogether. One painting

by the modern artist Marie Laurencin was appraised at $75. We sold it for $140,000. Most of the works were similarly undervalued. The appraiser generously offered to buy the estate for the appraised price!

The appraisal business has its share of disreputable types, so be on guard. One favorite scam is to tell you that your tarnished candlesticks aren't terribly valuable and generously offer to take them off your hands for $100. What the appraiser neglects to mention is that they are George II candlesticks worth $2,500.

Naturally, I have my prejudices when it comes to appraisers. It is really very difficult to match the auction house, which has a wide variety of in-house world-class specialists, each of whom has his finger on the pulse of the market every day.

If you do not have easy access to an auction house, however, there are a number of associations that can point you to a reputable appraiser. The largest of these are the American Society of Appraisers, the Appraisers Association of America, and the Art Dealers Association of America. Some of these organizations require qualifying exams, and others require a minimum of five years' experience.

Still, membership in these organizations is no guarantee of competency. It is up to you to determine whether this person has the requisite depth of knowledge and breadth of experience to do a solid job.

Before you put your potential appraiser to the acid test, be aware that appraisals have become highly specialized. The talented generalist who could appraise old masters and souvenir spoon collections with equal ease is now a thing of the past. First ask for a detailed rundown of his qualifications: How does his education and experience qualify him to evaluate a work? How long has he been in the business? How long has he specialized in this one particular area? Would he mind providing you with a reference list of past clients who were satisfied with his work? It might help if the references included a major bank trust department or a law firm that uses appraisers regularly.

Once you have selected a qualified appraiser, you will want

THE BEST OF EVERYTHING

to discuss with him the reasons behind the appraisal. A good appraisal will be based on the most current selling prices for comparable works. But the appraiser is free to use the somewhat lower figures from private sales and auctions or the higher figures from gallery sales, depending on whether you want a modest appraisal for gift tax purposes or a more generous appraisal to keep your insurance coverage current with inflation.

Although the term "fair market value" is sufficiently vague to allow for some creative thinking on the part of appraisers, there are minimum requirements for an appraisal that must be adhered to. In addition to a dollar figure for each individual item, a typical appraisal also includes a brief description of the object; any marks or signatures; its weight, height, and measurements; subject matter; medium; the name of the artist or craftsman; the date the work was executed; and the country of origin. A more thorough appraisal might also offer the historical importance, the provenance, and the exhibition history.

For items worth over $25,000, the IRS requires all this and more, including a photograph of the work, the date of acquisition, and an explanation of the factors upon which the appraisal is predicated—the state of the market, recent sale prices for comparable works, and so on. In the event of an IRS challenge, an appraiser, like a tax preparer, should be willing to back up his appraisal through the conference and appellate processes.

Appraisals need not be expensive. Bring an object to us, and our experts will offer a free oral valuation on the spot. Often someone will send us a photograph, and we will get back to him with a general idea of what the item pictured might bring at auction. Our experts at times have traveled around the country conducting what we call "Heirloom Discovery Days"—an opportunity for area residents who might never get near a major auction house to bring their treasures to us for a verbal appraisal for which a modest fee is charged, most of which goes to the local sponsoring museum.

For potential big-ticket items or large collections, auction houses charge a fixed fee, which is based on the time required to complete the appraisal, including travel, processing, and research. When the appraisal is done in contemplation of sale, should the property be consigned, a portion of the fee is usually refunded.

In appraising the appraiser, be demanding. But once you have hired him, don't interfere. Out of pride of ownership, too many collectors look over the appraiser's shoulder. They want the expert to tell them what they've known all along: that their collection is exceptional. If you pressure him, he just may cave in. As a result, you won't get the straight answers you need to put a realistic valuation on your property. So it is probably a good idea to butt out—just for now.

Once you have the typed, dated, and signed appraisal in hand, go over it carefully to make sure nothing has been inadvertently left out. It is possible that an object has somehow been overlooked—a silver-handled cane from your collection of nineteenth-century walking sticks, for instance, or that inverted airplane issue that is the cornerstone of your stamp collection. If this has in fact happened, ask for a correction. If certain evaluations appear to you to be way off the mark, now is the time to speak out. Ask the appraiser to explain how he or she arrived at this figure.

Once you are satisfied with your appraisal, stick it in a folder along with a color photograph of each item, then store the original report in a safe place—preferably a bank safe deposit box. Before you do, have copies made for yourself and the appraiser, and possibly your lawyer and accountant. If the appraiser has a file copy at his office, any updating can be done quickly and easily over the phone.

Shopping for Insurance

It is no small irony that while people with very small collections tend to be insured to the hilt, the big collector, faced with huge premiums, tries not to purchase a penny's worth more of insurance than he truly needs. Yet another group, who would never think of neglecting to insure their stereos and VCRs with a homeowner's policy, fail to consider the fact that their coin collection or the prints on the wall also require coverage.

For the 99 percent of collectors who do want adequate insurance but fall between the two extremes, there is no hard-and-fast rule governing how much or what type of coverage you should have. Each policy should be tailored to the individual's needs and desires, just as your rates will be determined by where you live, whether or not you have an electronic home security system, and a host of other factors.

Your comprehensive homeowner's policy automatically covers your personal property, the dwelling as well as all its contents, for a fixed sum. This includes, of course, any art, antiques, or collectibles. The standard homeowner's policy protects your possessions against the usual calamities: theft, fire, smoke, vandalism, wind damage, ice, sleet, hail, falling trees, flood, and so on.

The trouble with simply relying on your homeowner's policy as protection is that it makes little distinction between the bedroom lamp you bought at Macy's and the Tiffany Favrile glass and gilt-bronze lily lamp you bought at auction. You are left having to convince the insurance company that one is worth $75 while the other would cost $10,000 to replace. The situation gets even dicier when you try to explain that the ashes in your hand are what remains of your collection of Mathew B. Brady Civil War photographs worth $40,000.

For collections valued at less than $25,000, a fine arts rider added to your regular homeowner's policy should suffice. Over that amount, it is probably wise to take out a separate fine arts policy—"scheduled insurance"—that specifies each item. In both cases, you will want fair market value coverage. With this type of coverage, the insurance company accepts your appraisal(s) of the item(s) covered and pays you the full replacement value if you suffer a total loss.

Needless to say, you should report any theft, damage, or loss to your insurer immediately. It would not hurt to ask for an adjuster who has had some experience in this field. If you have suffered a total loss, you will submit a claim for the full replacement value of the object in question. In the event the object is damaged but repairable, submit a claim that includes the full cost of restoration *and* the loss in terms of the object's depreciation. That Miró print you bought two years ago will never be as valuable after it has been damaged and restored as it was in its earlier, nearly perfect original state.

Once again, insurance costs can be so exorbitant that sometimes collectors are more or less forced to sell—as in the case of John Whitney Payson and van Gogh's *Irises*. The rather typical rate of $10 per $1,000 can be prohibitive even for the middle-range collector who has over the years amassed a collection of antique furniture worth $50,000.

Just as every collection reflects the personality of its owner, every fine arts insurance policy should be tailored to the individual. And just as you must keep your appraisal up to date, you must also keep your insurance coverage current.

The Care and Feeding of Your Collection

Once you have made the commitment to acquire a work of art or other collectible, you become its custodian, its caregiver, its loving parent. This is a concept connoisseurs have no difficulty understanding, since nearly all true collectors invariably regard these objects as either dear friends or adored children.

The responsibility for the care and feeding of your collection starts with simple maintenance. The horror stories concerning masterpieces that have been virtually destroyed through an owner's negligence (remember my friend's faded Picasso drawing?) are endless.

Just a few random tips: *Never* hang a work of art over a working fireplace. Soot, smoke, and heat have ruined many an exquisite painting. Keep watercolors, drawings, and prints out of direct sunlight. Oil paintings on canvas, strangely enough, stand up well to changes in humidity, while paintings on panel do not. The least durable are pastels and charcoal works, which are easily smudged and can react unfavorably to the subtlest changes in temperature. These works should not be hung on a wall where they will be disturbed by a slamming door; even a slight vibration can shake the powdery pigments right off.

Don't use Fantastik or any number of other cleaners on bronzes, unless you're looking for a rather bizarre patina. Most people are aware that moisture from the bottom of a vase or a glass can stain fine furniture, but how many know that moisture also stains marble?

Short of hanging them on a wall, there is no foolproof way to protect your Oriental rugs from showing some wear. To minimize this damage, map out the traffic patterns in your home, then place the carpets out of harm's way. You might also try rotating your carpets the way you would your automobile tires.

THE ARTFUL COLLECTOR

Vacuum them carefully, and in the case of very fragile weaves, use a broom to brush in the direction of the pile.

Books, manuscripts, and in fact all works on paper should be kept away from moisture, direct sunlight, and heat. Incandescent lighting is better for books than fluorescent lighting. If you collect lace, Alençon and Chantilly require dry cleaning and should be stored in a cool place. Lace may be best displayed between two pieces of *glass*—not plastic, which can turn the fabric yellow. Oddly enough, even the most delicate ceramics are among the most resilient collectibles. There is little you can do to damage a $1 million Ming vase short of dropping it.

Consult a museum or auction house conservator on the best ways to protect your treasures from undue wear and tear. If conservators had their way, all collections would be housed in hermetically sealed cabinets, away from sunlight, heat, moisture, and small children. Most of us will be unable to adhere strictly to all the rules set down by conservators. Collectors want to enjoy their possessions rather than constantly worry about them. But a conservator can help you avoid the kinds of mistakes that can turn a treasure into a travesty.

Finally, there may be no better way to protect your collection than to display it with pride. That old adage "Out of sight, out of mind" really applies in this case. Objects stashed away in boxes or drawers invariably wind up being neglected or getting misplaced. Among the items Bob Arehart's family has tucked away and consequently lost over the years are "a chain and lock from a Civil War prison camp, and coins dating back to 1700 that my mother found under a tree in West Virginia. If they had been properly mounted and framed," he insists, "they would have survived time and the many moves made by a typical family."

Take proper precautions, but by all means put your treasures out in the open where others can enjoy them. That way you, like any concerned parent, can keep a watchful and loving eye on your "children."

Trading Up

One distinguishing mark of the great collector is his ability to sell his mistakes—to dispose of his earlier "lessons," if you will. Few can bring themselves to part with their very first acquisition, any more than a shopowner is inclined to part with that first dollar bill that hangs framed behind the cash register. That one nod to nostalgia excepted, objects acquired early in one's collecting career should be routinely reassessed as you hone and refine your tastes.

This is a lesson I would do well to learn. In all my years of collecting, I have divested myself only of a set of eight Regency dining-room chairs—and then solely because they were uncomfortable. But the most astute collectors do cull out inferior items.

This editing process often is prompted by personal growth. Maybe you have concentrated in recent years on Shaker furniture, and the American painted Windsor fan-back side chair you picked up at a barn sale in 1973 no longer suits your taste. It might bring over $1,500 at auction today—money you can set aside for that Shaker rocker you've had your eye on. Or you may have been smitten with that pair of Royal Doulton vases five years ago, but that was before you zeroed in on studio pottery as your true love.

You might also find that you have duplicates of a certain item. Where one glazed redware pot would suffice, you have four— and three of them are gathering dust in the back of a cupboard. Right there is another reason to think of paring down: these things take up room. Shelves bow and attic floors buckle under the weight of objects that once enchanted us. Not long ago, one of the finest collectors of American folk art implored us to auction one of his early acquisitions: a European rooster weather vane that had been languishing on the floor of his bedroom closet for years. Perhaps now is the time to take a second look. You might free up some cash and some space in the bargain.

Strategies for Selling

As with everything else in life, timing is all-important in the collecting game. It is more or less assumed that the savvy collector follows the market so that should the need arise, he will know the optimum time to sell. Sometimes this means striking relatively quickly. Other times this means waiting patiently for market conditions to heat up so that you can get maximum competition among potential buyers.

If you decide to sell through an auction house, you will benefit from the excitement and interest generated by each season. January, for example, is probably the best time for American and English furniture and the decorative arts. One reason: That is the month the annual winter antiques show in New York attracts thousands of collectors and dealers from around the country. The galleries are jammed, the mood is up, and people are eager to buy. Make it your business to know when the major sales in your particular collecting area are conducted so you can hop on the bandwagon.

For objects valued under $10,000, Sotheby's conducts frequent "arcade" auctions on the first floor of our York Avenue galleries in New York. These sales are fast, efficient, and designed to get the seller the best possible prices within one month of consignment.

For items valued over $10,000, the process is considerably less speedy. First, enough quality objects must be assembled in a specialized category to fill a catalogue. When those objects are selected for inclusion, they are meticulously researched and photographed. Then an international advertising and marketing campaign is launched to reach all potential buyers. Nothing is sadder than an object selling for half its rightful price because the one collector who would have bid a fortune wasn't even aware of the sale. In the end, it can take up to six months from the time a consignor contacts the auction house to the time the gavel comes

down. Most sellers don't mind the wait if it means they are getting the best possible shot at making a handsome profit. As one
leading collector put it, "Sell in haste, repent at leisure."

But how do you decide what is the best time to sell? Follow
the action in your collecting field, see what comparable items
are bringing at auction, study such relevant periodicals as
Antiques Monthly and *Connoisseur,* pore over the most recent
price guides to see where individual objects from your collection
stand.

When it comes time to sell, patience should be your byword.
If you see a major sale on the horizon, hold off. Just as the Stewart
Gregory auction in 1979 started a stampede in the direction of
folk art and the Duchess of Windsor sale in 1987 sparked an
interest in animal jewelry, major sales and exhibitions can be
counted on to stimulate subsequent interest and to boost prices.

English sporting paintings and prints—those lush, sprawling
landscapes populated by racehorses, fox hunters, and country
squires—spruced up the oak-paneled walls of many a fashionable home and club until World War II, when they came to be
considered somewhat stodgy and old-fashioned. Throughout the
fifties and sixties, these equestrian portraits plummeted in value.
Then, in 1972, George Stubbs's portrait *Baron de Robeck Riding
a Bay Cob* sold in London for over $250,000. That sale launched
a revival of interest in sporting art among English collectors, but
it would be another six years before *Antiques Monthly* declared
that sporting art was on the brink of a revival in America.

Smart owners of sporting prints and paintings read these
signs correctly and waited even longer to sell. In June of 1980,
Sir Alfred Munnings's *Start at Newmarket* brought $325,710.
Seven years later, we auctioned *Start at Newmarket* to an American collector for $1,210,000 and Stubbs's *Baron* for $2,420,000
—eleven times what it had brought previously. Sporting art is
back in vogue, spelling huge gains for those collectors who were
perceptive—and patient—enough to bide their time.

Late-nineteenth-century Chinese snuff bottles could be had

THE ARTFUL COLLECTOR

for $10 apiece twenty years ago. These same snuff bottles went up to several hundred dollars apiece, then inexplicably took a nosedive in the mid-1970s. Many collectors, fearing that previous price gains were illusory, bailed out.

Those who followed the market closely over time and *had the strength of their convictions* regarding the high quality of nineteenth-century Chinese snuff bottles held on. In 1982, a fine porcelain snuff bottle circa 1850 and signed Wang Bingron sold for $2,200. Five years later, just one month after the landmark auction of T. Y. Chao's collection of Chinese art in Hong Kong, that same snuff bottle brought $8,800 at Sotheby's in New York. With worldwide interest in Chinese art continuing on the upswing, the day after tomorrow might be the right time to sell, depending on when you got into the market and what profit you can realistically hope to gain.

Regardless of when you choose to make your move and whether you sell at auction or directly to a dealer or a private collector, you will want to present what you have to sell in the best possible light. Any object you wish to sell should be thoroughly cleaned. If it's silver you're selling, polish it first. Whenever possible, paintings should be attractively framed. Again, restoration is not always necessary; in fact, the wrong restoration can destroy the value of a piece. It's one thing to clean the dirt and wax buildup from an antique and quite another to strip off the original finish. If you choose to restore an item before putting it up for sale, consult an expert first. Basically, when it comes to showcasing your collectibles, a little common sense goes a long way.

Be sure to maintain accurate, up-to-date records, including recent appraisals, a detailed description of the object, a clear, close-up photograph (8 inches by 10 inches or larger), and if possible a recent list of prices earned for comparable items. That way, you'll be able to strike while the iron and the market are hot.

Collect Deep, Not Wide

All else being equal, a collection of ten paintings from a single period or artist is more highly regarded than ten paintings from ten different periods or artists. Victor and Sally Ganz focused their collection, zeroing in on Picasso and, when he became too expensive to collect, a handful of abstractionists. When a dozen pictures bring $44.8 million at auction, you can be sure that these represent the very best of the artists' work.

This is not to suggest that a great collection cannot be diverse. The treasure amassed by such varied collectors as the Garbisches and the Linksys, J. Paul Getty, Andrew Mellon, and Norton Simon —as well as Andy Warhol—was sweeping in both size and scope.

For those without unlimited funds, however, it is always preferable to specialize. The reasons for this are twofold. As you narrow down your interest in a field, you obviously have a better chance of becoming an authority on it. But you can also appreciate it more; as your depth of knowledge increases, so does your depth of enjoyment.

The pyramid process—starting with a broad base and building upward to a peak of excellence in the arts—ultimately separates the novice collector from the connoisseur. You might start out collecting smoking paraphernalia, narrow your focus to pipes, then zero in to collect meerschaums only.

You may also choose to narrow your area down in terms of geography, time, style, or all of the above. You start out with a general interest in antique furniture and wind up concentrating on Chippendale pieces made in Philadelphia between 1780 and 1800. Or you might collect objects of vertu—paperweights, portrait miniatures, Russian enamelware, mosaic plaques—before deciding to focus on paperweights exclusively. Not just paperweights, but paperweights made by Baccarat in the late nineteenth century. You can launch your career collecting every conceivable folk art item from quilts to decoys and discover that you are really enchanted by whirligigs.

John McDonough is the quintessentially focused collector. McDonough's lifelong interest in art began with his first visit as a schoolboy to the Toledo Museum of Art in Ohio and was intensified during his time as a medical student by the Art Institute of Chicago's great Impressionist collection.

Dr. McDonough set out with his first acquisition in 1965—John Singer Sargent's *Portrait of Mary Turner Austin*—to create a collection of American paintings spanning two centuries. The collection, noted for its breadth as well as its comprehensiveness and uniformly exceptional quality, was exhibited in major museums around the country before I auctioned it at Sotheby's in 1978.

Soon, Dr. McDonough grew restless. Within months he set out to form another collection of American paintings, but with a major difference. This time he confined himself to a fifty-year period, between 1875 and 1925. The result was a collection that, by virtue of its coherence, was even more impressive than the first.

In medicine, the law, and nearly every other area of human endeavor, this is the era of the specialist. The same is true for collectors. Do not make the common mistake of scattering your energies. Find the area you truly love, then devote yourself to it. Narrow your focus. Refine your taste. Your newfound expertise will show in the caliber of your collection and make you that much better equipped to really enjoy what you've got.

There are no easy answers, no tricks that will enable you to succeed at collecting without really trying. If you want to acquire art that will appreciate, then you must learn to appreciate art. This involves some considerable dedication on your part. You cannot learn to become a connoisseur overnight or from simply reading a book.

THE BEST OF EVERYTHING

What you have learned from this book is how to go about developing your expertise. You have seen that there is a definite method to the collecting madness—from determining the all-important nine criteria of value discussed here, to mastering the auction game, to educating your eye. Whether your particular passion is Degas, Dalí, decorative arts, or Disneyana, there is a correct way to go about collecting it.

You have also seen that when compared to alternative investments like stocks and real estate, art, antiques, and collectibles have performed phenomenally well in recent years. All indications are that this trend will continue into the 1990s and beyond.

In the final analysis, the best way to invest in art and antiques is not to invest in it—at least not in the conventional sense. You must collect with your brain, but you must also collect from your heart.

It bears repeating: Buy for love *and* money, but first for love. If you go about it the right way, you will undoubtedly discover that collecting can be incomparably rewarding—in every sense of the word.

Appendix

The following lists of associations and auction houses should give you some idea of the resources available in your area. As for reputable art, antiques, and collectibles dealers, there are literally thousands nationwide. Remember that finding a good dealer can be as important as finding a good broker. Before doing business with a dealer, an auction house, an appraiser, an artist, or a private collector, do some checking with the appropriate organization listed below and your local museum.

Associations

AAA	Appraisers Association of America, Inc. 60 East 42nd Street New York, NY 10165
AAAA	Antique Appraisers Association of America 11361 Garden Grove Boulevard Garden Grove, CA 92643
AADA	Associate Antique Dealers of America Box 8854 Indianapolis, IN 46208
AADAOPA	American Association of Dealers in Ancient, Oriental and Primitive Art 153 East 82nd Street New York, NY 10028
ADDLA	Art and Antique Dealers League of America 353 East 78th Street New York, NY 10021
AAM	American Association of Museums 1055 Thomas Jefferson Street NW Washington, DC 20007
ABAA	Antiquarian Booksellers Association of America 50 Rockefeller Plaza New York, NY 10020
ACAC	Association of Corporate Art Curators Box 11369 Chicago, IL 60611-0369

APPENDIX

ADA	Antique Dealers Association of America Box 335 Green Farms, CT 06436
ADAA	Art Dealers Association of America, Inc. 575 Madison Avenue New York, NY 10022
AFA	American Federation of Arts 41 East 65th Street New York, NY 10021
AIPAD	Association of International Photography Art Dealers 60 East 42nd Street New York, NY 10165
ASA	American Society of Appraisers Box 17265 Washington, DC 20041
FASA	Folk Art Society of America Box 8245 Richmond, VA 23226
GIA	Gemological Institute of America 580 Fifth Avenue New York, NY 10036
IACA	Indian Arts and Crafts Association 4215 Lead SE Albuquerque, NM 87108
ICSBS	International Chinese Snuff Bottle Society 2601 North Charles Street Baltimore, MD 21218
IFAR	International Foundation for Art Research 46 East 70th Street New York, NY 10021
IFPDA	International Fine Print Dealers Association 485 Madison Avenue New York, NY 10022
ISFAA	International Society of Fine Arts Appraisers Box 280 River Forest, IL 60305
NAAD	National Antique and Art Dealers Association of America 49 East 53rd Street New York, NY 10022
NADA	National Association of Dealers in Antiques 5859 North Main Road Rockford, IL 61103
USAA	United States Appraisers Association, Inc. 1041 Tower Road Winnetka, IL 60093
VSA	Victorian Society in America 219 South Sixth Street Philadelphia, PA 19106
WADA	Washington Art Dealers Association Box 50607 Washington, DC 20004

APPENDIX

Auction Houses

Arizona

Jack Sellner
Box 1113
Scottsdale, AZ 85252

California

Sotheby's
308 North Rodeo Drive
Beverly Hills, CA 90210

Joel L. Malter & Co., Inc.
Box 777
Suite 518
16661 Ventura Boulevard
Encino, CA 91316

Colonial Stamp Co.
Suite 202
5410 Wilshire Boulevard
Los Angeles, CA 90036

Richard Esterhazy Galleries
926/8 North La Cienega
Los Angeles, CA 90069

The J. M. Goodman Auction Gallery
Suite 10
1888 Century Park East
Century City
Los Angeles, CA 90067

G. Ray Hawkins Gallery
7224 Melrose Avenue
Los Angeles, CA 90046

Numismatic Fine Arts International,
   Inc.
10100 Santa Monica Boulevard
Los Angeles, CA 90067

K. C. Self, Jr., Auctioneer
53 Victory Lane
Los Gatos, CA 95030

John Moran Auctioneers
3202 East Foothill Boulevard
Pasadena, CA 91107

Butterfield & Butterfield
220 San Bruno Avenue
San Francisco, CA 94103

California Book Auction Galleries
Suite 730
965 Mission Street
San Francisco, CA 94103

Neale & Sons, Inc.
Box 425
14320 South Saratoga-Sunnyvale Road
Saratoga, CA 95071

Art Deco Auctions Ltd.
19528 Ventura Boulevard
Tarzana, CA 91356

Connecticut

Canton Barn
79 Old Canton Road
Canton, CT 06019

Nadeau's Auction Gallery
489 Old Hartford Road
Colchester, CT 06415

Collectors Auctions Ltd.
Box 2207
Danbury, CT 06813

Litchfield Auction Gallery
Route 202
Litchfield, CT 06759

Mystic Fine Arts
47 Holmes Street
Mystic, CT 06355

APPENDIX

Robert H. Glass Associates, Inc.
Box 237
Sterling, CT 06377

Auctions Unlimited, Inc.
The Resale Company
4 Surf Road
Westport, CT 06880

Woodbury Auction Service
661 Washington Road
Woodbury, CT 06798

Arman Absentee Auctions
Box 174
Woodstock, CT 06281

Washington, DC

John W. Kaufmann, Inc.
1333 H Street NW
Washington, DC 20005

Adam A. Weschler and Son, Inc.
905 E Street NW
Washington, DC 20004

Florida

Glentiques Ltd.
Gary Kirsner Auctions
Box 8807
Coral Springs, FL 33075

Arthur James Galleries
615 East Atlantic Avenue
Delray Beach, FL 33483

C. B. Charles Galleries
Suite 6
750 East Sample Road
Pompano Beach, FL 33064

William James Alquist Auctions
Sanibel Island, FL 33957

Georgia

Red Baron's Antiques
6320 Roswell Road
Atlanta, GA 30328

Depew Galleries
1860 Piedmont Road Northeast
Atlanta, GA 30324

Lenox Auction Gallery
5070 Peachtree Industrial Boulevard
Atlanta, GA 30341

Illinois

Joy Luke
300 East Grove Street
Bloomington, IL 61701

Chicago Art Galleries
20 West Hubbard Street
Chicago, IL 60610

Hanzel Galleries
1120 South Michigan
Chicago, IL 60605

Leslie Hindman Auctioneers
215 West Ohio Street
Chicago, IL 60610

Howard Art Galleries, Inc.
600 North Wells Street
Chicago, IL 60610

Rare Coin Company of America, Inc.
31 North Clark Street
Chicago, IL 60602

Dunning's Auction Service, Inc.
755 Church Road
Elgin, IL 60123

Pick Galleries, Inc.
886 Green Bay Road
Winnetka, IL 60093

Indiana

Kruse International
Box 190
Auburn, IN 46706

Richard Waskow
Box 2123
Michigan City, IN 46360

APPENDIX

Louisiana

Ace Auction Company
Hunt Auctioneers
1621 Cameron Street
Lafayette, LA 70506

Neal Alford Auctions
4139 Magazine Street
New Orleans, LA 70115

Morton Goldberg Auction Galleries,
Inc.
3000 Magazine Street
New Orleans, LA 70115

Roberts Orleans Auction Galleries
701 Magazine Street
New Orleans, LA 70115

Maine

C. E. Guarino
Box 49, Berry Road
Denmark, ME 04022

James D. Julia Auctioneers, Inc.
RFD 1, Box 91
Route 201, Skowhegan Road
Fairfield, ME 04937

Morrill's Auctions, Inc.
Box 710
Gray, ME 04039

Richard W. Oliver Auctioneers
Box 337
Route 1, Plaza 1
Kennebunk, ME 04043

Robert Foster
Box 203
Newcastle, ME 04553

F. O. Bailey Antiquarians
141 Middle Street
Portland, ME 04101

Maritime Antique Auctions
RR 2, Box 45A
York, ME 03909

Maryland

Theriault's
Box 151
Annapolis, MD 21404

Harris Auction Galleries, Inc.
875 North Howard Street
Baltimore, MD 21201

Old World Mail Auctions
5614 Northfield Road
Bethesda, MD 20817

Waverly Auctions, Inc.
Suite AA
4931 Cordell Avenue
Bethesda, MD 20814

C. G. Sloan & Company, Inc.
4920 Wyaconda Road
North Bethesda, MD 20852

Alex Cooper Auctioneers, Inc.
908 York Road
Towson, MD 21204

Massachusetts

Robert W. Skinner, Inc.
Route 117
Bolton, MA 01740

Grogan & Company
890 Commonwealth Avenue
Boston, MA 02115

Rose & Cleaves, Inc.
488 Harrison Avenue
Boston, MA 02118

Robert W. Skinner, Inc.
2 Newbury Street
Boston, MA 02116

James R. Bakker, Inc.
370 Broadway
Cambridge, MA 02139

F. B. Hubley & Co.
364 Broadway
Cambridge, MA 02139

Carl R. Nordblom
Box 167
Harvard Square
Cambridge, MA 02138

Richard A. Bourne Co., Inc.
Box 141
Corporation Street
Hyannis Port, MA 02647

Caropreso Gallery
136 High Street
Lee, MA 01238

John C. Rosselle Co., Inc.
The Auction Gallery
182 Cherry Street
Middleborough, MA 02346

Janis Aldridge, Inc.
7 Center Street
Nantucket, MA 02554

Pioneer Auction of Amherst
169 Meadow Street
North Amherst, MA 01059

Sandwich Auction House
15 Tupper Road
Sandwich, MA 02563

Bradford Auction Gallery Ltd.
North Main Street
Sheffield, MA 01257

Michigan

Frank H. Boos Gallery
420 Enterprise Court
Bloomfield Hills, MI 48013

Du Mouchelle Art Gallery
409 East Jefferson Avenue
Detroit, MI 48226

Stalker Galleries
2975 West Maple Road
Troy, MI 48084

Minnesota

Rose Galleries, Inc.
1123 West County Road B
Roseville, MN 55113

Missouri

Pavilion Galleries
Box 216, Route 2
Joplin, MO 64804

Robert Merry Auction Co.
5501 Milburn Road
St. Louis, MO 63129

Selkirk Galleries
4166 Olive Street
St. Louis, MO 63108

Montana

Stan Howe & Associates Auctioneers
4433 Red Fox Drive
Helena, MT 59601

Allard Indian Auctions
Box 460
St. Ignatius, MT 59865

Nebraska

Kaufman and Dolezal Auctioneers
1235 K Street
Lincoln, NE 68508

Nevada

Stremmel Auctions
121 Vesta Street
Reno, NV 89502

New Hampshire

Paul A. Buco
Auctioneer and Appraiser
617 Main Street
Danville, NH 03819

Sanders & Mock Associates, Inc.
Auctioneers-Appraisers
Box 37
Tamworth, NH 03886

APPENDIX

Sanders Auctioneers
Route 101
Wilton, NH 03086

New Jersey

Berman Auction Gallery
33 West Blackwell Street
Dover, NJ 07801

Allan Nixon Auction House
167 Arney's Mount
Pemberton, NJ 08068

Brownstone Mill Auctions
74 Godwin Avenue
Ridgewood, NJ 07450

New Mexico

Stephen's Gallery
Consignment and Auction
2701 Cerrillos Road
Santa Fe, NM 87501

New York

Gantz Auction Gallery
307 Railroad Avenue
Bedford Hills, NY 10507

Bob and Sallie Connelly
666 Chenango Street
Binghampton, NY 13901

Doyle Auctioneers and Appraisers
Box 137, RD 3
Fishkill, NY 12524

Gilvert Auctions
Alldone
Garrison-on-Hudson, NY 10524

Christie, Manson & Woods,
    International, Inc.
502 Park Avenue
New York, NY 10022

Christie's East
219 East 67th Street
New York, NY 10021

Christie's–Robson Lowe
502 Park Avenue
New York, NY 10022

William Doyle Galleries
175 East 87th Street
New York, NY 10128

Harmer Rooke Numismatists Ltd.
Harmer Rooke Galleries
3 East 57th Street
New York, NY 10022

Harmer's of New York, Inc.
14 East 33rd Street
New York, NY 10036

Lubin Galleries, Inc.
30 West 26th Street
New York, NY 10010

The Manhattan Galleries, Inc.
1415 Third Avenue
New York, NY 10028

Phillips Sons & Neale, Inc.
406 East 79th Street
New York, NY 10021

Sotheby's
1334 York Avenue
New York, NY 10021

Swann Galleries
104 East 25th Street
New York, NY 10010

Tepper Galleries, Inc.
110 East 25th Street
New York, NY 10010

Pleasant Valley Auction Hall
Box 173, RD 2
Pleasant Valley, NY 12569

Rinaldi Auctions
133–135 Bedell Road
Poughkeepsie, NY 12603

Herman Darvick Autograph Auctions
Box 467
Rockville Centre, NY 11571

APPENDIX

F. E. S. Auctions, Inc.
9 Park Lane
Rockville Centre, NY 11570

Ohio

Fordem Galleries
10322 Lake Shore Boulevard
Bratenahl, OH 44108

Main Auction Galleries, Inc.
137 West Fourth Street
Cincinnati, OH 45202

Judy Robinson Art & Auction Gallery
3500 Columbia Parkway
Cincinnati, OH 45226

Wolf's Gallery
1239 West Sixth Street
Cleveland, OH 44113

Oregon

O'Gallerie, Inc.
228 Northeast Seventh Avenue
Portland, OR 97232

Pennsylvania

Hartzell's Auction Gallery, Inc.
RD 2
Bangor, PA 18013

Lansdowne Auctioneers
11 South Lansdowne Avenue
Lansdowne, PA 19050

The Fine Arts Company of Philadelphia
2317 Chestnut Street
Philadelphia, PA 19103

Samuel T. Freeman & Co.
1808 Chestnut Street
Philadelphia, PA 19103

South Carolina

Charlton Hall Galleries
929 Gervais Street
Columbia, SC 29201

Texas

Garrett Galleries, Inc.
1800 Irving Boulevard
Dallas, TX 75207

Heritage Numismatic Auctions, Inc.
311 Market Street
Dallas, TX 75202

Steve Ivy Philatelic Auctions, Inc.
311 Market Street
Dallas, TX 75202

Hart Galleries
2311 Westheimer Road
Houston, TX 77098

Utah

Olson Auction Galleries
4303 South Main Street
Salt Lake City, UT 84107

Vermont

Duane E. Merrill
32 Beacon Street
South Burlington, VT 05401

Virginia

Samuel Yudkin & Associates
2109 Popkins Lane
Alexandria, VA 22307

Shields Auction Galleries, Inc.
Box 5143
1515 West Broad Street
Richmond, VA 23220

Washington

Satori Fine Art Auctioneers
2305 Fifth Avenue
Seattle, WA 98121

Wisconsin

Milwaukee Auction Galleries
318 North Water Street
Milwaukee, WI 53202

APPENDIX

Schrager Auction Galleries Ltd.
Box 10390
2915 North Sherman Boulevard
Milwaukee, WI 53210

Travis Auction Galleries
1442 Underwood Avenue
Milwaukee, WI 53213

Barretts Auction Center
4120 8th Street South
(Highway 13)
Wisconsin Rapids, WI 54494

Index

Page numbers in *italics* refer to illustrations or graphs.

INDEX